"What a rich life it is to have these memories of time spent with the young Azmari singer Tigabu, the Lalibela poet Tilahun, and the other spirits of improvisation. I envy Itsushi Kawase. For him the streets of Gondar are close, dear, and touching."

—Ryuichi Sakamoto

Mischief of the Gods:
Tales from the Ethiopian Streets

Itsushi Kawase

Copyright © 2023 by Awai Books
All rights reserved
Book design by David Matthew Davis
Translation by Jeffrey Johnson

ISBN: 978-1-937220-11-2
Original Japanese edition published by Sekaishisosha. Copyright © 2018 by Itsushi Kawase. All rights reserved. English translation rights arranged with Sekaishisosha.

Exclusive rights for English publication licensed to Awai Books 1178 Broadway 3rd Floor №1062 New York, NY 10001

Mischief of the Gods:

Tales from the Ethiopian Streets

Itsushi Kawase

Translation: Jeffrey Johnson

Prologue 9

Spirits of the Piazza 14

You, the Sun's Lullaby 22

Mulu's Snake 32

China the Egg Vendor 38

Song Pleading with the Gods 50

Chaplin of the Highlands 58

A Symphony 68

The Promised Land 76

Eternity 86

Mischief of the Gods 96

Qolo Temari 104

A Promise to Yohannis 114

Reacquainted 124

Journey 132

Elder Brother's Way 138

The Crucifix 146

The Ethiopia Hotel 154

Epilogue 165

Notes 166

Contents

Prologue

I chased clouds. Baked in the sun, blown by the wind, I played my instrument as if possessed. I surrendered to its violent rhythms, setting myself free from all that defined me. I yearned to go beyond all boundaries, to lose sight of myself. Travelling across African borders, playing with local musicians, those days undoubtedly left their traces. Long ago I decided to study anthropology and felt drawn towards researching music. And then Africa came to me of her own volition. I was given an opportunity to do my fieldwork in Ethiopia. I had never been to the continent. My meager knowledge was limited to vague links between Africa and the kinds of music I loved then—blues and jazz.

This book is mainly set in Gondar, a historical city in the north of the Ethiopian Highlands. My encounter with the city dates back to the year 2001. I had left Japan, traveled via Cairo, days after the 9/11 terrorist attacks in the US, arriving in Addis Ababa, the capital of Ethiopia. With a guitar strapped to my back, my purpose was to conduct fieldwork. I took long-distance buses, plagued by fleas and ticks, and travelled across a vast African plateau. I heard along the way that there were traditional musicians and singers in the north. I gradually headed in that direction and eventually, as if carried by a current, reached the city of Gondar. It is the ancient seat of the king and home today of the *Azmari* musicians. They are story chanting bards who play stringed instruments in ritual festivals and at bars. I immediately decided on this city as the base for my research and settled in at a cheap room in Ethiopia Hotel, a remanent of the Italian occupation.

In Gondar I collected stories. Some people spoke eloquently, some of them in whispering tones. I'd close my eyes, listen, tell the voices to slow down, to relax, be calm. The utterances of these streets would resound in me, well up and overflow. These voices did not pertain to the fact-based discourse that I, as an anthropologist, am trained for. Nonetheless, I try in this book to give them voice. At times, they find expression in fragmentary pronouncements and monologues, at other times they pretend to be dialogues, or somewhere between thought and speech. They are in an indeterminate style, straddling poetry and prose, or sometimes just a poorly written short story. I give stylistic form to these discourses as appropriate, hopefully conveying the life-changing narratives that left such a profound impact on me and others.

For me to understand, I needed to destroy my culturally determined conception of 'music', smashing it to bits with a hammer. Musicians in Gondar were considered an artisanal group along with tanners, weavers, blacksmiths. The majority of the inhabitants of Gondar are members of the Ethiopian Orthodox Church, its solemn ritualistic music and hymns are considered gifts from God and sacred. Then there are the Azmaris with their secular music who are looked down upon as socially inferior. They work the streets.

The roads of Gondar are endless. The episodes of this book connect Gondar to North America, Europe, and Japan. The extension of the streets is brought about by displacements of the people and myself. The roads are the matrix of people's daily lives, the theater of their self-expression, where they survive. They may welcome you hot or reject you all together.

Welcome to the streets.

Prologue

1

The Spirits of the Piazza

In the Piazza of a bustling Gondar shopping district, artists scratch out a living plying their trades. All kinds of performances take place as the musicians try to earn money. There's more attention to collection than to the art on display. One such artist is a guy who goes by the name 'Joker'. He plays an Ethiopian *washint* flute. With the street bustle as orchestral backing, one can hear as if from afar the flute playing a *tezeta*, pentatonic scale in a major key. Joker repeats a single melody while the city buzz softens, then a calm descends. Joker ekes out a living in a few hours on the streets moving from place to place playing his flute and collecting tips.

Then there is the whistling teenager Gedamu. With his hands at his mouth, he produces a whistle from his throat, creating unique, mysterious sounds. He accentuates them by simultaneously tapping his cheeks with his fingers and pauses by cutting the air off with his tongue. On the Piazza and streets there are other youngsters like Gedamu who make money whistling. All are blind. They hitchhiked to the city from villages at the foot of the Ras Dashen Mountains, more than 100 kilometers from Gondar. If they make it to the Piazza they can scratch out some kind of living even if they are blind. I heard from his cousin how Gedamu lost his vision: 'After a long drought, it rained, steam rose from the earth and Gedamu was blinded by *mich*'. Mich is Amharic for diseases caused by the sun. The common treatment is to drink medicinal tea made of plants such as haragressa and damekase.

Beggars are usually called *lemagne*. This is the most common expression for them that derives from the word 'to beg'. One will also often hear the euphemism, *Emebete*, which is also a name for the Virgin Mary, the central figure of the Ethiopian Orthodox Christian Church. It is the place of worship for the majority in northern Ethiopia. So Emebete has the nuance of someone to be pitied yet under the patronage of the Virgin Mary. The people of Piazza also refer to beggars as 'the spirits of the Piazza'—*ye piazza qole*. The beggars or street spirits are not only ridiculed or looked upon with pity, they are also recognized as beings outside normal social controls, as well as part and parcel of this cityscape.

A woman known as Attū is a renowned character among the spirits of the Piazza, she might best be called 'Queen'. Her outlandish personality makes her stand out among the many spirits in and around the Piazza. Prematurely aged, Attū is also deaf. She makes a living on her movements: she stoops, lumbers in, forcefully grabs the arms of passers-by, reveals one of her drooping, wrinkled breasts and pantomimes breastfeeding a baby. She badgers people for money making the claim that she has a baby to feed. Passers-by know that the elderly Attū has no babies. The choice one has, is to pay homage to her compelling performance, or be overwhelmed by her presence—specifically her odor, a wild stench that emanates from every pore of her big body. I offer her some spare change.

When Attū grabs my arm, I grab hers. Although her demonic countenance does not change, she stops badgering people and shouting, she seems to calm down a bit, tucks her breasts into her clothes, and heads off in search of her next target. One day out of curiosity I touched her face, she thought I was making fun of her and made as if she were going to punch me but just turned and walked away.

When evening falls some street urchins show up to poke fun at her. They imitate Attū's gestures, voice and posture of exposing a breast and feeding the baby. Attū lets out a shrill cry, anger flows through her and she pelts a barrage of rocks at those little shits in fits of rage. Attū cannot throw at all so the large, slow-moving Attū's stones don't just fail to hit those nimble brats, but hit people rushing home after work in the evening. For passers-by it's quite an annoyance, but viewed from the sidelines it's very comical. I, myself, scolded the boys although I held back countless times. But this time Attū seems desperate and her chasing street urchins is a rather typical evening scene on the Piazza.

Attū is a nickname—no one I've met knows her real one. A masculine pronoun from the local Amharic, *anta*, means 'you', and that is what she calls the passers-by who she thoughtlessly grabs by the arm. Coincidently, anta sounds just like the Japanese second-person pronoun, you. But she mispronounces the word so that it sounds like she's saying 'Attū, Attū'. This is evidently how she came to be called just that, Attū. However other than uttering this word, she does not engage in what could be called conversation; she gestures, moans, and screams as she accosts those she encounters on the street.

Attū's stench is horrendous, indescribably powerful. I often hear the word *atala* in cheap bars. Atala refers to the sediment that collects at the bottom of vessels used in the production of *tella*, a local liquor made by brewing sorghum or teff (a grass of northern Africa). In my mind atala is the accumulation of the street people's desires, sorrows, and dreams in concentrated form. It has absorbed and accumulated and fermented even further—and this is her smell.

Attū often defecates in crowded streets in broad daylight. She picks up the excrement using newspaper to move it out of the center of the street. When I first saw this I was stunned, but for the people of Piazza, Attū's private act in public does not shock at all, they just pass by looking nonchalant.

One wonders where Attū came from? What sort of place does she call home? Does she have family? The people of the town say that Attū was married to a soldier. In that past was Attū a housewife who could hold a normal conversation? How is it that she end up begging in the street like this? It is said that Attū has sons and one of her grown-up sons apparently makes ends meet delivering liquor and food to restaurants. When Attū is ridiculed and teased in the evening, has her son ever come to defend her by throwing stones at her persecutors? Is her Piazza performance that includes a childrearing bit really just a performance? On some level of her own reality could there be a baby that needs nurturing and protection.

At some point I began to fantasize that Attū and the spirits of Piazza were a link between the streets and an otherworldly realm. They are a portal to an endless, something like a deep tunnel. People tip Attū not out of pity, but out of awe at the deep sanctuary she is a manifestation of a realm that people cannot casually access. The image of Attū begging has become an integral part of Piazza in the afternoon for me. When I don't see her, I feel empty and I search asking those working the streets shining shoes or following other pursuits, like the street urchins, where Attū went today.

One day Attū suddenly disappeared from Piazza. Piazza suddenly became thin, open, inorganic and uninspiring. I asked the street people where she had gone but no one knew. Then one day the word on the street was that a taxi driver she was close to had said Attū was living in a welfare facility on the outskirts of Gondar—an institution that exclusively for disabled people run by a foreign NPO. I was curious about Attū so I bought flowers and visited the facility. At the end of a neat pavement on the grounds of the facility was an orderly, well-maintained flowerbed.

I asked the staff at the facility about visiting Attū, and they replied that it would be alright. After waiting for quite some time, Attū came out of her room. Her hair was cut short and she was wearing a clean light beige coverall dress. I thought her ogre-like countenance had softened and she was calmer. Above all that indescribably strong odor had disappeared, and she was clean and neat. I guessed that it was the staff of the facility who were taking care of her. I offered her the flowers and she went to take them but hesitated, looking confused and looking as if she didn't know what the gesture was or meant. I gave her my blessing, said goodbye, and I was about to leave when she threw the flowers on the ground and grabbed me by the arm. Then she suddenly revealed one of her breasts and made a pose asking me for money. A great sense of relief spread over me.

2

You, the Sun's Lullaby

You rise slowly from your cardboard bed off to one side of the street and let out a big yawn and stretch. Standing still and looking into the sky the morning sun slowly warms your whole body. Yes, just stand there, that way the cold air of the street that you inhaled during the night will soon be replaced by the gradual warmth of the morning sun. This is your morning ritual. Gondar's capricious and mischievous sun and wind sustain you. At times and in certain situations they can be a scourge to those they take exception to and cause myriad diseases. But the morning sun is different—it accepts and affirms all, gives energy to move through the day. Well, 'what shall we do today', you think, right in the middle of town under the Pepsi billboard in the Piazza district.

Borko (dirty, pig), *Duriye* (rogue, ruffian), *Godana Tedadari* (child on the roadside), *Baranda Lijoch* (child under the eaves), and *Adegegna Bozene* (probable criminal) are some of the names given to you and your friends by people whose view of you who live on the streets is colder and harsher than the cement of the streets where you bed down at night. But the police officers patrolling the streets, roaming drunks, and the brutally violent thieves, who target you and your money as they too sleep in the streets, are of far greater concern than the opinion of the greater, polite society surrounding you.

You and your ilk who live on the streets, where in the world did you come from? The background and circumstances are various. Some have been separated from their families due to conflict, famine, or HIV. But there also are those who simply hated working on a farm and felt a vague attraction to life in a city. Looking for work in Gondar is all well and good but in the end many couldn't find a job and ended up living on the streets.

Even you children can engage in various occupations on the streets. When you just arrived in this town you first sold beans. As vendors children go from bar to bar to sell beans that go well with drink. Then there's barley, roasted with a little salt spread in a colander and sold. Boiled chickpeas kneaded with mustard powder can be sold. In addition, kids sell mandarin oranges, tissues, limes, eggs, candles, tobacco, lottery tickets, gum, powdered juice, bread, potatoes, and firewood. You sold so many things, more than you can even remember.

After that, you became a *listro* (shoeshine boy); right here under the Pepsi billboard. Before going to work adults would have their shoes cleaned. First they were washed with a cloth soaked in water and detergent, then polished with a cream applied by brush. Depending on the condition of the shoes, there were minor repairs done, such as on holes and the soles. In the Piazza district here, there are multiple listro groups that compete for shoe customers and territory and there was constant fighting between them.

Next for you was to work as a *wellettō* (a type of street vendor). This was done by holding a square paper box in front of your chest. In it biscuits, tissues, chewing gum, cigarettes, condoms, candy, incense, matches, lighters, hair styling products, and household goods are spread out. With this you move around the city at night conducting your sales business. You learned to enjoy the taste of tobacco when you started this job. One notch above wellettō is to display and sell watches, belts, underwear, socks, etc. on a wooden board as tall as you are; but you haven't gotten that far yet, have you? Why? It's because you got addicted to *qumar*, gambling with juice bottle caps. Oh yes, sometimes loaded and unloaded the luggage of bus passengers. You also worked as a *tashakami* (hauler of goods) carrying alcoholic beverages purchased at restaurants and bars to stores. You also made a little money by washing cars parked on the street and guarding parked cars. You don't approve of vices such as smoking and gambling. You're really a hard worker.

When you didn't have time or couldn't eat, you'd wait in front of a restaurant in the Piazza district and pick up the discarded leftovers before the stray dogs could get them. Also Gondar has forty-four Orthodox churches where food is served to people on the feast days of the churches associated with Medhanialem (Savior of the World), Michael (Saint Michael), Gabriel (Saint Gabriel), Maryam (Mary), Abbo (Abune Gebre Menfes Kidus), and God and other saints. In the evening after the prayers, beggars gathered around the churches to partake of *sinde dabbo* (bread), and *injera* (Ethiopia's staple food made mainly from the cereal teff), and the local alcohol, tella. If that isn't enough you can go to Mr. Bete, the dry cleaner. People speak ill of Bete, in exchange for giving money and food to children like you, he takes advantage of you sexually pawing at your bodies. I honestly don't know if it's just a rumor or if it's true.

One day, three seasoned ruffians taught you how to pick pockets dexterously using only your index and middle fingers. Early the very next day near the bus station, you took about nine 100-birr notes and the ID from the pocket of a middle-aged woman. Of course, you were a little nervous and hesitant at first but once you tried it, you felt that it was nothing to be concerned about. It was very easy. Your friends urged you to spend all the stolen money. Your heart was beating fast. You spent about a hundred birr on food. Afterwards for some reason, you were tormented by remorse. You searched for the old woman's house and ended up honestly confessing to stealing her money and returned the remaining 800 birr and her ID. You were again worried and thought she might send someone for the police, then the police would beat you mercilessly. But to your surprise, she didn't turn you over to the police. She said, 'May God bless you always". She was very sincere in giving her blessings and introduced you to her children.

After leaving her house, you went straight to Saint Abbo Church and begged forgiveness for your sins. You swore to Abbo that you would never steal again. Abbo Church is named after your favorite Saint. His full name is Abune Gebre Menfes Kidus. Abbo is amazing, he came to Ethiopia from Egypt. Abbo lived in the wild and was adored by many animals. It is said that Abbo's body was covered with hair like a beast. The main thing that fascinates you about Abbo is the fact that in his 500 years Abbo never ate or drank. As a child, he did not drink his mother's milk or water. When Abbo was five hundred and twenty-five years old God said, 'now it is time for you to leave this world'. At this of all times is when Abbo exerted his willpower and rejecting the notion that he should die. Of course God was angry. Jesus himself was crucified, so why shouldn't Abbo face his own death with bravery? Abbo replied that he himself didn't have a reason to die—why he hadn't yet enjoyed the fruits of living in this world, he hadn't received the earth's blessings. You love to ruminate on this strange conversation between God and Abbo, a conversation you heard from a monk when you were just a kid.

You stood at the entrance of the bus station and carefully examined the young people coming to this town. You breathe in the winds they bring from Addis Ababa, 730 kilometers away. Sometimes you envy stylish young people who sport trendy hairstyles and wear fashionable clothes. At times like those it seems reasonable to invest some of your hard-earned money to try to look good in trendy outfits. But you know in just a few days—no just a few hours—that hair and those clothes would soak up the soot and grime and return you to the same streets. Never mind that all you have to do is run down the Qaha or Angereb River and wash your clothes while you're bathing. It's that simple.

Just don't let your guard down and relax at the bus station. It's a den of pickpockets and rogues. Kangaroo is the leader and for you he may be a troublesome opponent. Kangaroo's real name is *Gebre Kristos*, Servant of Christ. What a pompous and depressing name! The Kangaroo uses a wooden cane, wraps his crippled and undeveloped right leg around the cane like an ivy, and hops down the street—that is why he is called Kangaroo.

Kangaroo stakes out bus stations to catch foreign tourists who have just arrived in Gondar by long-distance bus. And, in his poor English, regardless of whether it is fact or fiction, he talks in rapid succession about his underprivileged upbringing. Taking advantage of the other person's sympathy and pity for him, he asks for spare change. He also introduces tourists to hotels, grocery stores, affordable restaurants, and historical sites. He supports himself with commissions he gets from merchants. He's from the same streets as you and like you, Kangaroo often works the bus station area. He clings to you and spits on you. You want to avoid that irritating bastard if you can. But he'll always come out of nowhere and hurl abuse at you. Just this evening he pretended to throw a stone at you from across the road, right? Saying to you, 'Hey, asshole, how much did you earn today? Huh? You're shitting me, right?'

But you can never forget that time when kangaroo was trying to build a cardboard house for a little stray kitten. It was around the time when the rainy season had passed and the yellow daisies, which symbolize the Ethiopian New Year, began to bloom. It was hilarious to see homeless Kangaroo living in the streets but building a house for a dirty, skinny feral kitten covered in mud. You had never seen Kangaroo look so kind, and it made you feel very uncomfortable and strange. He noticed your gaze and gave you an awkward look but immediately, as usual he glared at you, clinging to his cane in the rain hopping away.

Between jobs you sometimes set foot in a *Video Bet*. The place overflows with heat and the stench of sweat. Yet, you and your acquaintances lose yourselves staring intently at a TV monitor. For a very minimal fee you can spend hours watching various videos and films. Television and the Internet are not common in households in this town. Some Video Bets are open in the living room of a house to show recorded TV footage, while others rent out a town cafeteria for a certain period of time and broadcast sports by satellite. Thugs who hatch evil plots and are given to fighting call a temporary truce to spend time in these Video Bets. Those living as beggars, mendicant monks, and those aspiring to become clergy can also be found at Video Bets. Even you and Kangaroo could probably meet under a temporary ceasefire (or maybe not).

Video Bet is your most precious sanctuary. Middle Eastern melodramas, Hollywood action movies, Hong Kong kung fu movies and more. You can understand the obvious duel scenes and car action scenes, but you do not perfectly understand the Arabic and English exchanged in serious dramas. You give your own interpretation of the characters' facial expressions, gestures, and demeanor and do so in a whisper so as not to disturb the other people. It's not just about passively enjoying the videos.

You imitate the movements of MTV hip-hop and Ethiopian popular music artists, who create new songs and dances that mix Amharic and English, as well as using coined words. You never miss a match from the English Premier League. If your favorite Arsenal wins, you go out into the open at once, form a circle with all the Arsenal fans, and triumphantly return to town while chanting the name of your team. You drink in the sounds and images with your whole body, you respond and resonate with the world, and shout it out to the streets.

When you're exhausted and fighting hunger, you always think of Abbo who never drank or ate. And you always grumble to yourself in your heart—well now when you die, you will argue with God; you didn't enjoy the fruits of this world either, so there's no reason for you to die. But wait, it hasn't been all that bad, has it? At the same time, you think you have to take good care of yourself. And you are being watched over.

2

You, the Sun's Lullaby

3

Mulu's Snake

Is it a stain or is it a painting? It has no beginning and no end. Blue, red, white, yellow, purple, green, countless dots scattered everywhere. While the colors complement each other, they each emit their own radiant light, twisting, swelling, and coiling. They begin to illuminate first the street's and then the world's every nook and cranny. I am blinded by the light.

A pointillist drawing by a beggar woman named Mulu is in my notebook. My hotel room is frequented by all types, from beggars to musicians to homeless children, and also the dubious self-proclaimed 'street guides' who get change giving 'tours'. Mulu is one of my frequent visitors. Her eyes widen like a *Nio* (temple guardian deity). A kind smile plays around her lips as does praise around her mouth. She wears a dark skirt with soot and mud stains. Judging from her appearance, she must be in her late forties, but the townspeople say she forgot her age long ago and will always remain a girl.

Mulu tiptoes with her upper torso leaning forward slightly. It gives her the appearance of floating as she comes and goes. There is some incomprehensible purity about her that cannot possibly fuse with the mass of confusion that is this city and its people—something that floats along unperturbed—that is Mulu. She appears out of nowhere, then just as suddenly disappears somewhere. For some reason the street urchins don't try to pull their pranks on her or mess with her at all.

When Mulu comes near my place she shouts 'you, you' in a high-pitched voice. I am not sure if she thinks you is a term of address for foreigners or just for me. But there she is, and she looks down the street and then peers up towards my rented room. When I greet her she shyly looks away, bows her head, and silently climbs the stairs into my room. When I welcome her she doesn't look me in the eye or talk to me but sits in a chair with her head down and picks up my field notes. Then with some pens that are on the table she starts making lots of dots endlessly, endlessly. The dots eventually become lines, then snakes that begin to undulate, she goes on like this page after page. Mulu and I have hardly ever spoken to each other. She stands serenely scrawling something in my notebook as time flows along peacefully. Then little by little my sensations and memories turned inwards to the image of a boy playing in a country river.

It's early summer. Cicadas cry at sunset in a basin valley. You can smell freshly drained rice fields. Then, suddenly, a numbness permeates the first joint of my right index finger. I am good as can be at catching snakes with my bare hands. You hold your breath and slowly approach

34 | *35*

the snake, grabbing it by the tail is not the way to do it. You aim for the neck and tighten the fingers of both hands on the neck. The snake emits a strong smell that makes you want to turn your face away as it resists the grasp I have on it—or perhaps more precisely it is repelled by the very existence of humans. Once I got the hang of catching snakes I caught blue snakes, striped snakes, black crow snakes, and tiger keelbacks with my bare hands. I raised them at home too. On my way home from school, I held snakes, hid them in shrines, and passed by schoolmates feeling both threatening and proud. But I had never caught a pit viper. I was well aware of the visibly poisonous markings and the danger of the triangular-headed serpents, and that they gave off a peculiar fishy odor unlike any other serpent.

One day, when I was playing in the river with my neighborhood friends, I saw a pit viper coiled at water's edge. In my foolishness I was motivated to seize it to show off in front of the friends who were there. As usual, I approached softly and quickly grabbed the snake by its neck. I easily caught it and in that moment of pride—a sharp numbness ran down the first joint of my right index finger. There was no pain at all just complete numbness. As soon as I got to the village clinic, the doctor examined the fang marks on my finger, and curiously, he said the fang marks were not those of a pit viper. In the middle of the night my hand from fingers to wrist became paralyzed and the backs of my hand, my arm had turned purple and swollen to twice their normal size. Now from my hand to my shoulder the arm was intensely hot. I had a fever, sweat profusely and it felt as if my right arm had separated from my body. I was taken to the hospital in an ambulance, where I was injected with an antidote serum—that saved my life. After that, I thought my index finger was going to rot away but the swelling subsided after a few weeks. Yet, the bones of my fingers were forever disformed and looked to have partially melted. My index finger was and is slightly bent to the right. The neighbors seem to have enjoyed my pain 'that naughty, naughty little shit finally got his just what he deserved'. Even now, when I throw a ball it veers to the right and first joint of my right index finger is bent and inflexible.

Whenever Mulu visits my room within a certain amount of time the old man who is the innkeeper inevitably comes with his cane and pulls Mulu by the shirt to lead her out to the street. How he hears or finds out she is visiting, I don't know. Nor do I fully comprehend his objection to me inviting Mulu into my room. Meek and quiet Mulu never did anything untoward. But Mulu's pointillist ceremony bothers him. When she leaves she'll squeeze a sound from the back of her throat, or other times as if it was only natural to disappear she takes her leave without saying anything, just goes out of my room, down the stairs with hardly a sound and slips out as if getting sucked back out into the streets. Mulu's snake remains as she left it, incomplete in my notebook—well, maybe this was intended, maybe it as complete as it should be.

As I travel from country to country, I often come across snakes in mysterious places. Artists and scholars who have worked with me often tell stories of dreams they had of snakes. A silhouette artist from Istanbul, who provided me with the music at one point, says that he imagines a snake swimming gracefully across a river. When the snake crosses the river, flowers bloom on both sides. A dancer from Montreal says that a snake slowly crawls up her spine while she dances and climbs over her head, her hair will then bear different kinds of fruit. A historian at the University of Addis Ababa said she saw snakes swimming in the air before and after a seminar she co-hosted with me. Gondar has a ritual of possession called *zar*. The mediums for zar are mostly women, and it is said that they dream night after night of mating with a giant serpent. The vision-dream is always seen during zar as the medium begins to be possessed by spirits and transform into human to spirit.

One day Mulu was hit by a large truck in front of my hotel and died in a sea of blood. It happened when I was on business in the neighboring town for a few days. Mulu may have been on her way to create pointillist snakes as usual in my field notes. Her snake drawing is unfinished. It's been a long time since Mulu died. In my memory she has the eyes of a Nio and a gentle smile on her lips. When someone opens the notebooks Mulu's snakes soar high into the sky, scattering the hustle and bustle of the street, the dust, the smells and colors. The coiled scenery in my memory still shakes me inside. Even if she turns into a snake, Mulu will still be doing her pointillist drawings in my notebook— endlessly, endlessly.

3

Mulu's Snake

4

China the Egg Vendor

The sky howls suddenly and opens to a heavy rain that pounds the earth creating a muddy brown stream flowing through the streets. It seems the rain gulps down people's desires and washes them away. The people on the street whose work is interrupted by the rain for a while click their tongues and mutter but knowing in their hearts that this rain will bring blessings to the farmers and eventually to them. While evacuating to hide under the eaves of shops and huddled together they stand there glaring at the gray sky.

In thirty minutes, the rain stops as if nothing had happened, the sun that had been hiding returns. After being washed away the world emerges again with clear outlines, catches the sunlight and begins to breathe powerfully.

A boy who is a tour conductor on a minibus raises his high-spirited voice trying to get more passengers. Street vendors carry crates of sweets and cigarettes and move into the streets. A beggar girl sheltering from the rain takes her blind mother by the hand and peers fearfully into the tavern to see if there are any potential customers. A group of shoeshine boys making up lost time move their bodies rhythmically while polishing customers' shoes. The streets of Gondar are full of working children. The street is the mother of their economic activities and the theater where they can boldly give expression to their fight for survival.

Early in the evening just before night falls is a very dear time of day to me. *Shir shir* (strolling) those people wandering around without purpose, just go back and forth along the street to chat with friends and acquaintances, meet, report on what happened today, check on each other's current affairs. 'How is your child? How are your father and mother? How were the store sales today?' It is also good to ask about relatives or work, or silly gossip about acquaintances is also fine. The real purpose of shir shir is neither to collect information nor to maintain the daily chatter that is the basis of smooth neighborly relations. No, in the first place, the word 'purpose' is not suitable. For some reason just reconfirming your connection with people, feeling their warmth, then drifting into the twilight that is shir shir, shir shir.

One night when I was hanging out on the street, a girl with pale skin and Asian shaped eyes named China appeared with a light blue bucket full of boiled eggs on her shoulder. She ran up to me, asking me to buy some eggs. When I said 'I don't want eggs', she immediately said 'not for you, for me'. So I ended up buying two, one for her and one for me. She peels her shell quickly and deftly with one hand. Another girl,

Sanait, about China's age, comes running over with a bucket of boiled potatoes as if it's only natural to do so. She sometimes pesters me to buy potatoes. China carefully opens a piece of newspaper to give me some salt. Her hair smells like cheap soap.

China's forehead is tattooed with a cross typical of rural women. The cross signifies her affiliation with the Orthodox Church. With a playful look, she recounts how she got her tattoo which was done by a village tattoo woman—a middle-aged woman who did everything from tattoos to hairdressing. The raw material for tattoo ink is the soot that comes from burning tires. This soot is dissolved in water and mixed with the liquid squeezed from the leaves of plants used to prepare the black ink-like liquid. This 'ink' is used to draw patterns on the forehead, neck, chin, and elsewhere. A razor-sharp needle pierces the skin, letting the ink soak in. Of course this is painful. To keep her from crying out in agony, her mother made little China swallow down *araqe*, a local alcoholic spirit. She says that when she drinks, she forgets the pain. Since that time she has been drinking and even smoking. China sits at the edge of the road between selling eggs. For some reason the image of her smoking a cigarette with a cold expression rid her of a hick smell, and gave her a dignified air, making her look older than her actual age. Was her heavy makeup unbefitting a girl in her mid-teens? It was intended to hide the cross on her forehead which townsfolk deride as the mark of a rube.

China often asked me to take her to Japan. When she didn't get an answer, she took her light blue bucket and ran off with a loud laugh. It wasn't until much later that I found out that China, while in the egg-selling business, was also selling herself.

At a much later date as I was walking through Gondar, I heard a familiar voice calling me. It was China who was now an adult. She ran a small café, the opening of which had been funded by a German patron. It was located right next to *Fasil Ghebbi* (Fasil fortress), one of Gondar's most popular tourist attractions. China, who had grown taller, wore a national costume and she held a coffee ceremony for me to celebrate our reunion after ten years. The coffee ceremony is an important daily ritual that is symbolic of the spirit of Ethiopian hospitality and is performed by women. China rambled on to me while I drank coffee. She had worked in the Middle East for a while.

She said Riyadh, Saudi Arabia is really bad. She became a maid of a merchant family there. Women from numerous locations, Indonesia, Philippines, Bangladesh, and Ethiopia go to Riyadh to work. Employer violence against these women, unpaid wages, and various problems routinely occur. Indonesia and the Philippines have put pressure on the Saudis at governmental levels to improve the poor working conditions for their workers, as a result, in recent years it has become quicker and more convenient for employers to hire unprotected workers from Ethiopia rather than those from Southeast Asia. In China's case, her passport was seized and held by a broker upon exiting the airport. The head of the household assaulted her and even sexually harassed her. The master's wife sensed that her husband was turning his attention to China, became very jealous, and began to treat her harshly. With the support of her friends from the streets in Ethiopia, she managed to escape with her life but returned home empty-handed. Through a contact she made in Riyadh, she worked at a restaurant in Addis Ababa. Subsequently, she got involved with a German guy who frequented the restaurant, became her boyfriend, and they married. He seems to help her out a lot.

There is an Amharic proverb, *Qes beqes Enqulal BeEgru yihedal,* which means that the egg eventually turns into a chick and little by little walks—this means that you have to take your time to achieve your goals or to accomplish something—this also implies that the process requires patience. When I complimented her on how impressive she had become, referring to the proverb. She chuckled, 'I'm still an egg'. There are still times when China's innocent smile comes to mind, accompanied by the warmth of shir shir, and the cool of an egg shell that has sucked in the cold night air.

4

China the Egg Vendor

5

Mischief of the Gods

Song Pleading with the Gods

God is a weaver
God is bad at weaving
As he weaves he unravels

This is a verse from a song offered to God from amidst the clamor
and cigarette smoke of a bar. A boy steadfastly sings, with his gaze
fixed on the empty space in front of him. He plays the stringed *masenqo*.
He furrows his brow and lifts his chin slightly. The old men at the
bar continue to chat, the boy raises his voice oblivious. The melody
spins out directionless, but his voice is powerful. It can't compete
with the heat and noise in the crowded tavern on a Saturday afternoon.

The boy's name is Tigabu, born *Azmari*, a formerly noble caste of professional musicians who served the court by entertaining. Azmaris long acted as court musicians to the nobility, in a role that encompassed that of clown, political agitator, social critic and spokesperson for commoners. Close to power and sometimes in resistance to it, they played an important role from olden times—somewhat akin to the role of jesters of other cultures.

Tigabu roams from tavern to tavern. He steadfastly sings, whether entangled with drunks or ignored by customers. First he shows something of his Azmari roots by singing a song in praise of the gods that also expresses the fleeting nature of life and the impermanence of this world. Gradually he picks up the tempo by following up with a love song about Gondar, and leads into a eulogy with extemporaneous poetry. No matter how excited customers may be, the performer remains as stern looking as ever.

Everyday life for an Azmari is not easy. They are despised by the public, and are understood to be in a category of *moyategna* (craftsmen), who also include blacksmiths, tanners, pot makers and weavers. Intermarriage with moyategna is generally avoided. Worse yet, in everyday conversation the word Azmari means a beggar or someone who speaks nonsense, and is used to slander.

Tigabu with a musical instrument on his back, is sometimes the object of ridicule. The stringed instrument masenqo is a tool of his trade and indicates to people that Tigabu is Azmari. A resonator of goat skin, a tube of hard wood, sticks to beat the resonator, strings of bundled horsetail hair, and a bow made of curved olive wood define him and can leave onlookers with a negative impression. It can be quickly dismantled when traveling by bus and easily hidden in a thin cloth bag, then reassembled when on the street.

When he wanders from bar to bar in pursuit of an opportunity to sing, if he is found out by adult Azmaris who protect their own territory, the mid-teenage musician will be chased away. Even if he finds a place to play it is rare for a boy with mediocre performance skills to be paid a lot in tips.

Today is market day. A group of farmers who come on foot from the villages at the outskirts of the city once finished selling their grain in the morning, sip *mead* (a liquor made of fermented with honey, water and shrub) and seem content. Outside the tavern the crop-hauling donkeys too are off duty and stand motionless. A group of five or six old men gather around the injera and chat excitedly.

Before long Yitayal also joins those at the tavern. He is an Azmari boy the same age as Tigabu. Yitayal sits at a distance from the group of old men with his instrument on his lap and he gazes intently at Tigabu. Yitayal had been at a nearby bar and from the way he looks the tips must not have been good. Just by looking at Yitayal's expression Tigabu can tell that he didn't receive a penny. Only a year ago, Yitayal made up his mind and started attending the town's elementary school. However, because of his Azmari ancestry, he was ridiculed daily by his much younger classmates so he quit school and returned to the streets. Tigabu and Yitayal come from an Azmari village thirty kilometers south of Gondar. They stay in the center of town in an area for low-income people, living at an inn where they rent a room behind the Piazza. The area was a so-called red-light district during the period of Italian rule and is crowded with cheap bars. Prostitution is rampant. Drunken brawls and thefts are a constant. The two of them live in a very cheap place where farmers from distant rural areas stay in the city for the weekend. A thin goat skin cushion called *agoza* is laid on the dirt floor and a rag-like blanket is draped over the head to sleep. The agoza comes complete with fleas and ticks. Tigabu and Yitayal have been in arrears for some time even if the cost per day is less than the cost of a glass of local liquor. The landlady complains to them every day saying that they will have to vacate soon.

A well-built man in the center of the group loudly makes delicious sucking noises enjoying the marrow from his mutton bones. Tigabu aims for this powerful looking old man while singing and playing through his own hunger. He swallows his saliva. He steps into the line of vision of the old man to try to captivate him. He repeats a short melody on the masenqo and calculates the timing to start singing. He beats out the rhythm with his left foot. Seeing through Tigabu's strong gaze and intentions, the old man looks back with a sullen look, makes a gesture to go away as if shooing away a dog or cat. The old man smells of the sweet and sour odor of fermented honey (mead), that is, of someone who is drunk. Tigabu immediately asked the man his name and who was with him. Of all things, apparently the old man's name is '*Adana*'. He starts to sing:

Adana, your humorous stories are loved. There are no bees in your stomach, but your mouth is overflowing with honey

This 'honey song' is pleasant. The lyrics indicate that Adana is a good talker, a pleasant person and this softens him up a bit. But still looking dubious, the old man turns to Tigabu, claps his hands, and takes up the rhythm moving his shoulders. He lets himself loosen up to the song. Watching the old man slowly dissolve his wicked demeanor, Tigabu thinks that this is his chance. Watching the old man's reaction carefully, Tigabu continues to sing.

Let's make Adana laugh, so we can count among his 30 teeth, the gold ones.

A gold tooth is a symbol of affluence. So he used the word to create the impression that this old man is wealthy. Of course, if you change the name of the person you are singing to, the lyrics will work for anyone. This old man, Adana, had no gold teeth, but his dingy smile glistened and he began to giggle and dance cheerfully. Tigabu takes heart at the sight of the old man enjoying his song. However, no matter how much he sings, no matter how much he praises old Adana, there is no sign of him tipping Tigabu. It is customary for the person being sung to to express gratitude by sticking some denomination of Birr (Ethiopian currency), on the singer's forehead. A numb Tigabu paused several times to tap his bow on his forehead and gesture to the customers for a tip. While sending cold glances over Tigabu's gesture, the crowd quickly returned to chatting as if nothing had happened. The guests at the bar drink with each other as if Tigabu isn't even there. A waitress carrying mead opened her mouth wide and in a hoarse voice tried to say something to Tigabu. He thinks to himself that she can't hear him very well, but he's had enough of playing and will go somewhere else. Tigabu clicked his tongue and stopped playing. Then he turned to Yitayal and gave the signal with his eyes that it was his turn.

Putting masenqo on his lap, Yitayal lightly rubs the strings bundled in horsetail hair with a pumice stone. He waited for his turn to perform, but seemed reluctant to get up. His voice is weak and unreliable, the strings sound pluckless. He attempts a friendly smile to the guests. Yitayal, who lacks confidence in both singing and playing, is good at coaxing percussion out of the masenqo. While plucking the strings with the index finger of his left hand, he drums the goatskin resonator with his bow. But the old people gathered there still do not listen. He thinks 'These assholes are nothing but drunkards. My heart must be cold. I want out of this place immediately'. Yitayal communicates with Tigabu by using Azmari 'jargon', a kind of code woven into the lyrics. The coded messages are like wordplay; minor tricks like reading words backwards or twisting consonants. Even so, if such vocabulary is interspersed in a conversation, it is completely incomprehensible to others. Azmaris use this kind of jargon or code strategically to their advantage in everyday conversation as well as in performances.

'Hey, let's go to the fortress. There must be a lot of foreign tourists visiting today', says Tigabu. 'Well, even if we go to such a place the guides will try to block our way and eventually drive us away. Let's go to another bar', Yitayal answers. Reluctant to go along with Tigabu, Yitayal speaks in code, as Tigabu steps out of the tavern into the street.
As you pass the giant fig tree of Jan Tekele Park, you will see the royal palaces and fortress built by successive emperors during the Gondar period. It is no exaggeration to say that these giant trees and fortress, which are often mentioned in Azmari songs, along with the names of historical heroes, are the heart of the proud Amhara people of the north. Long ago royalty and aristocrats would be accompanied by their favorite Azmari and have them sing songs of praise at banquets in fortress and at nights in camps. There are also Azmari who have been honored by the kings for their martial prowess, and who have received vast lands as rewards for their singing.

As they go along passing the fortress and approaching the crossroads of Piazza from the other side of the road a few street urchins yell and mimic the appearance of masenqo players. 'Azmari, Azmari, Azmari!' 'Why keep singing even though people despise me?' Such unanswered questions boil in Tigabu's mind. At that moment he remembers a story his mother told him about the origin of Azmari from childhood.

The old and sick Virgin Mary lays on her deathbed dreading the moment of her impending death. God tells Mary that death comes equally to all people and that she should not fear. As Mary approaches her death, God calls the angels Ezra and Dawit. He orders Ezra to play masenqo and Dawitt to play the lyre. They sing, 'No matter what you try, death comes to everyone.' Ezra and Dawitt continue playing and Mary completely forgets her fear of death and met her death as if falling asleep.

Among the Azmaris, it is widely rumored that they are descendants of the Angel Ezra. This allusion to their origins is also sung in the devotional song used at the beginning of every performance. The Azmaris, even if ostracized and ridiculed by society at large, envision their story, which affirms the sanctity of the group—their own validity reinforced through songs they listen to and recite.

Loud music flows from the speakers in the music shop. Thick synthesizer melodies and rhythms almost drown out masenqo sounds. However, the dialogue between men and women is splendidly developed in quick succession, with metaphors of historical sites and place names of Gondar, such as Fasil Ghebbi and the Ras Dashen Mountains symbolized as lovers. A poster on the door of the store shows a smiling Azmari couple in dazzling white folk costumes. A duo of Mr. and Mrs. Azmari singers represent northern Ethiopia. A boy stands just below the speakers, listening intently. He doesn't own an instrument, but he is Azmari and from the same village as Tigabu and Yitayal. Young Azmaris listen to songs on the radio and in music shops, memorize the lyrics, and allude to them in their own songs and performances. The Poster couple live in Gondar and nightly run a tavern called 'Azmari Bet', which specializes in Azmari music. I often hear their singing voices on the radio.

For the Azmaris who wander from bar to bar, it is a goal to work as an exclusive singer for Azmari Bet and earn a stable income. Envied by many Azmaris, the Azmari couple are usually in demand at wedding banquets. However, Tigabu and Yitayal do not think well of the couple, who are also distant cousins. Wedding feasts are held outdoors in white tents, and not only can you earn a lot of tips from happy guests, but you can also get free food. The couple are always the first to shun these two who sneak in and try to perform. Azmari adults, who have a strong sense of territory, are much more troublesome for Azmari children than the slander of drunken adults in bars.

Looking at the poster Tigabu convinces himself that one day he will become a singer who surpasses these two—he tells himself, makes conscious note of it, and raises his fist in salute to that thought.

At the entrance to the fortress walls Azmari children form a line and wait for the foreign tourists who come out of the fortress after their tour, of course, they are there to get tips. Zememu, the youngest girl in the Azmari ranks, is 7 years old. She holds a bundle of yellow daisies which are the symbol of Ethiopian New Year and gives them to tourists. As if it were a matter of course, Tigabu and Yitayal join the ranks of the other children. They begin to repeat the simple melody played on the masenqo. Several men among the tourists come out of the gate and walk toward the jeeps lined up to transport them. The children speed up their performances in an attempt to get the attention of the tourists. Some girls put out flowers. But the tourists just smile at the children, pass them by and get in a line to board the jeep. Everyone stands stunned as they stare at the vanishing jeep. Tigabu's hunger made his stomach growl. Recalling that he hadn't eaten properly for a day and a half, he gives up and runs up a small hill a short distance from the fortress. Far to the east Lake Tana floats faintly visibly and far to the south a huge rocky mountain bathed in the setting sun shines divinely. Tigabu throw down his instrument and lays down on the hill.

Ezra played the masenqo, Dawitt played the lyre, the Virgin passed away peacefully freed from her death throes.

The angel Ezra sang to ease the pain of the Virgin Mary's death. Muttering a song to the gods in a low, low voice as if it were a spell Tigabu took a deep breath, closed his eyes, and continued.

God is a weaver
God is bad at weaving
As he weaves he unravels

The lyrics compare the act of weaving to life and death that God gives to all things. God gives (weaves) one life after another, but at the same time he also takes (undoes the weave) of life in giving death. The verse can be taken as fatalism, resignation about death, or it can be taken as a satire on God who always takes life in giving death. Tigabu sings this lyric many times and momentarily it seemed that this was not his voice, an earthly voice, but there was a sensation of the sound coming from a world far, far away.

6

Chaplin of the Highlands

I hear a mysterious singing voice calling me from afar, it casts no spell, doesn't howl like the wind, yet comes to me from a tremendous distance, a place where space and time are undifferentiated. I have encountered such a singing voice before.

A young man draped in a thick cloth moves at a rapid pace as he travels from town to town in the Ethiopian Highlands. Even before the sun rises, he moves quickly from house to house, visits and sings. The young man's name is Tilahun. Perhaps because he has visited many areas, he sings in multiple ethnic languages. One day, he suddenly appeared hanging around in Gondar, and as if possessed by the singing voice of this young man, I followed him on a journey for a time, going from house to house and town to town.

You are as beautiful as honey and as open-hearted as a lake
Now keep your eyes on me
You are beautiful as a jewel
Respect from your neighbors and the blessings of many calves go to you Say 'go ahead', prove my luck, give it to me, prove my wealth
God's grace allowed us to meet
As long as death does not part us, we will meet again

Tilahun is a kind of wandering minstrel called *Lalibelloch* (*Lalibela* or *Hamina* in singular). They go solo or as a male and female pair, traveling extensively across Ethiopia, singing under the eaves of houses early in the morning, giving blessings and departing. The injera received at the door is thrown into a plastic bag that Tilahun carries. After he receives money, clothing, and leftover food, Tilahun gives the person a salutation beginning with the specific phrase: *Egziabhere Yistilegn* (May God provide you with multiples). He boldly sings a chorus of praise to the giver of money so that the neighbors can easily hear it, and steps away from the house. His song of praise in a dramatic and exaggerated tone gradually fills the surrounding space.

May God provide you with multiples
May God provide you with multiples
May you be free of woe
God bless you
As God heard the voices of apostles and prophets
You listen carefully, too
Give me a pillow because I'm tired, leaning
Since I'm not feeling well, let me get up
There is a country that can invite us without hesitation
May God guide you to that country, heaven
And bless you till the end of life

These verses or prayers to God are transmitted by raising one's palms toward the sky and repeatedly mumbling 'amen, amen'—this is the way to receive blessings. Tilahun is obstinate in his pursuit of patrons. He often obtains information about the person to whom he is singing from neighbors and incorporates it into his lyrics. This information includes the name of the person he sings to, the religion, occupation, family structure and other such matters. The lyrics are intended to lift the mood and urge the listener to give.

For example, in the early morning before going to elementary school children fill buckets with water and wash their faces at the eaves of the house; women cook breakfast over charcoal in front of their homes; Tilahun appears and asks, 'who is the owner of this place?' The person he asks is surprised and puzzled by his sudden appearance but feels compelled by the forcefulness of the Tilahun's inquiry so she blurts out the name of the owner. Suppose for example, that the name of the owner is Hussein, the name is clearly that of a Muslim. In cases where the religion is not discernible, Tilahun cautiously checks whether the owner of the house is Muslim or Christian. Then, he asks about the homeowner's occupation. Let's say Hussein is a merchant. Tilahun will repeat endlessly, 'O Hussein, follower of Allah, O Hussein, follower of Allah'. Then, he names some Muslim pilgrimage sites in Ethiopia and sings lyrics about *khat*, green leaves with stimulant properties that Ethiopian Muslims consume during rituals. Then he begins singing lyrics exaggeratingly praising the business acumen of merchants, 'a man who makes a hundred into a thousand' (with a small amount of capital produces great profits). If Hussein turned out to be a soldier, he could sing, 'A brave hero with many soldiers under his command'.

In response to the sudden visit by a Lalibelloch, the owner of the house rubs his sleepy eyes standing at the front door, and may wear a sullen look on his face at first. However, as Tilahun's clever songs appeal to both his vanity and his religious beliefs, the wariness and discomfort he held, peel away one by one and optimally, the homeowner will peel away and hand over banknotes.

In the early morning sleepy but bustling hustlers sing loudly at the entrances and under the eaves of houses. Of course some residents are angered and some chase away Tilahun telling lies: 'the owner of the house is sick', or 'most of the family is away at church'. But Tilahun does not give up at this. He responds comically and supplely to the cold-hearted. He drains the tension out of the situation. In part this is achieved by including their reactions in his impromptu song. To a housewife with a suspicious look on her face he sings 'Hey look here princess with such a sour look on your face, it's hard to see your beauty through that stark mask'. Of course, people's skeptical eyes are also on me, a suspect *ferenje* (foreigner) holding a camera and standing behind Tilahun. 'Who is this guy and what the hell is he doing with you?' people ask Tilahun who immediately sings, 'I'm supposed to sing in Japan soon, and this Japanese music producer just saw me for the first time'. Occasionally, there are those who invite Tilahun into their homes and treat him with kindness, but that is rare. Sometimes even if he sings continuously members of the family may not come out at all. The house remains completely silent and it's hard to tell if anyone's really there or not. At such times, Tilahun may sarcastically sing, 'Silence is the place where people are punished'. He sings on, 'Like a pregnant woman on the point of giving birth, I am restless, don't make me wait', and 'There, go ahead, demonstrate my luck, attest to my wealth'. Also under these circumstances, he gradually induces charity saying euphemistically, 'Here you go, prove my good fortune, here you go, prove my wealth'. Here you go—coaxes them to generously hand over money, clothes, and food to the singer. If he sounds like he's a hard-selling salesman, the exquisite push-pull bargaining in the interaction between Tilahun and others—should be more accurately thought of as a splendid performance of street theater.

'Don't forget to sing at the *Tezkar*'. Tezkar is a memorial service for the deceased. Lalibelloch are summoned to the Tezkar to sing songs in honor of the deceased. Here, too, careful research goes into the occupation and personality of the deceased in advance and get incorporated into the songs. While listening to the song the bereaved families cry for the deceased. It is customary to give the leg of a cow to Lalibelloch in gratitude for the songs. I can see Tilahun walking in front of me with this meat on his shoulder. The word *moya* that Tilahun uses includes not only singing skills, but also interaction and bargaining with people. 'Just as a funeral director brings his son to the burial site and teaches him various things, we learn from childhood by following our parents practices'.

There is a superstition that if the Lalibelloch ceases his professional activities he will contract *qomata* (leprosy), and fear of illness forces them to continue in these activities. There are multiple legends about the origin of the Lalibelloch.

One of the legends is the story of Gebre Kirstos. Long ago there was a young man named Gebre Kirstos. He decided not to marry and to live as a religious man with his only loyalty to God. Just then, Gebre Kirstos' parents tried to force him to marry a woman. The embarrassed Gebre Kirstos runs away on the day of the ceremony. But his parents send many messengers to catch him and bring him back to his wedding. Knowing that he is being pursued, Gebre Kirstos begs God to turn his skin inside to deceive his pursuers. Immediately his limbs began to rot and in no time at all no one could recognize him as Gebre Kirstos. Years pass and Gebre Kirstos returns to his parents' house. They do not realize that this man is their son. His mother takes pity on his diseased appearance, the terrible skin disease and puts him in a hut near her house to let him rest and gives him food every day. One night, Gebre Kirstos is summoned to heaven by angels. His parents find a piece of paper in the hut, the message on it indicates the man was their son and they grieve deeply.[1]

He was a son who was full of pure faith in God and lived only by receiving alms. Relatives and descendants vowed to God to remember Gebre Kirsto and live by begging. Another story goes like this, when God created the world the Lalibelloch ancestors who were supposed to be included were busy eating. God was angry with them for coming late. He then decreed that if his descendants did not continue to sing, they would be destined to be afflicted with a disease that causes the skin all over their bodies to rot.

In the above story the origin of the group's singing for alms is in connection with God. Opinions of the Lalibelloch themselves about the qomata legend vary. Many, including Tilahun, think it's just a hoax and nothing to fear. My wish for all the Lalibelloch is that the qomata and the other lie-filled superstitions, would simply disappear. It is not uncommon for the public to unilaterally assign a silly discourse to minority groups that enhance the discrimination practiced against them. But why do Lalibelloch keep singing? It is the fear of the qomata that really drives the group to continue their early morning activities? I wonder if there are other singers in other cultures these days who are restricted by such legends. Tilahun sometimes told me to speak my mind, let out my feelings. However, there are times when it seems that the discrimination against Lalibelloch is a case of an actively exploitive, frightening image that majority population hold against a certain minority group. When Tilahun is active in his practice, he covers his whole body with a thick cloth, loosely wraps the cloth around his head, and walks with a wooden cane. The sight of him slipping out of nowhere at dawn and starting to sing is eerie. However, around noon, Tilahun returns to the cheap hotel where he stays, changes into jeans and a t-shirt, and goes back to being a fashionable young man walking around the Piazza. Then he goes to a bar where he drinks mead, and spends a leisurely afternoon drinking with people. Of course, no one knows that this is the singer who had been roaming the streets until just a little while ago, dominating the morning air with the overwhelming power of his voice.

Mead is served in your house, and milk is served when there is no mead
May there be many heroes like you
May there be many children like you
you give people fat and mead

Tilahun's singing voice echoes in the cold air of the twilight evening on the plateau. His breath is white. He's singing right in front of me, yet his voice seems to come from somewhere in the distance—in the depths of my heart, his voice overlaps with another voice, also from a distant world. Those singing voices accumulate symphonically—they suddenly and naturally come in a surging accompaniment.

I once stayed in a room in a small youth hostel in northern Germany where I participated in a film festival. The man who shared the room with me, Gary, was a former chief of an indigenous people called the Dane-zaa of British Columbia. Gary said he went through a period when he was addicted to drugs and alcohol and suffered a lot. He managed to survive by facing his heritage, struggling to understand the Dane-zaa myths, language, wisdom of the land and the powers of the prophets of his people. He taught himself studying paintings, giving performances in bands and a virtual museum website. However, no matter how he tries to transmit the knowledge to the younger generation of Dane-zaa, they show little interest in Dane-zaa culture and their own heritage.

Gary and I went drinking together every night. Back in the hotel room, he snored so loudly that he kept me awake. In spite of that he woke at 5 am every morning and started his drumming and chanting ritual. He holds a hand drum lined with moose skin in his left hand, and a stick in his right hand, and he bangs on and on and on. Along with the rhythm, he groans, singing a song that may or may not have had lyrics. Gary receives messages and visions in his dreams night after night. Visions from gods and ancestors that he sings first thing in the morning. Of course, I don't understand the details of the song, and I didn't know anything about the Dane-zaa tribe until I met Gary. However, the singing voice and the simple beat of the drum, are not specific to the space of a small room in a town in northern Germany where we were present, but resonate from a distant world where past and future are indistinguishable. It gave me the ungrounded conviction that the music resonates from beyond our material experience. Occasionally that kind of sound visits me like a stranger, and invites me to a place where time and space are undifferentiated.

God's grace allowed us to meet again
Unless death separates us, we can meet like this
You were kind since childhood
Your body may wither, but your heart is still young

'Don't just suddenly yell in front of a private house or to the neighbors who pass by. First you greet them with a smile, 'Long time no see, how are you?', and then start singing'. Even so there are times when the residents lash out at singers and treat them like stray dogs. At such times perhaps out of concern for me when he too was feeling down, Tilahun would say 'Charlie Chaplin,' mimicking the comical gait of the comedy king, and jumping up and down in front of me. Other times, when I get more tips than I expected, I would make a mischievous face as I walk behind, and make the very same gestures while flashing the tip money.

Tilahun dreams he'll stop working as Lalibelloch and instead sing with a pop music band and be active in that world. A master of his language, he recounts his dreams in raps that he composes in Amharic. The morning after rapping his dreams, 'Chaplin of the Ethiopian Highlands' dreams of being freed from God's curse. But then, he decides to visit another house to tell them of God's good graces.

You are as beautiful as honey
May God bless
A world full of happiness and misfortune
God fills the void
Get home safely from work
Keep away from people's malice
May love surround you

7

A Symphony

Prayer 1

Inhale deeply then hit the bell hard. The whole body is bound in sound and reverberations. The sound of the temple bell at dusk spreads throughout the village. A great white heron nests in the trees of the shrine and responds to the bell with a noisy voice that doesn't sound at all like that white, pure and dignified figure the bird cuts. The dogs in the neighborhood howl excitedly as if they were chasing the vibrations. The sound echoes in the mountains and disappears in waves. Hit it again and again. The act of hitting the temple bell every day was a routine when I was young. The sound of the bell continues to pulse in my body. Sometimes it suddenly comes up from inside me in Gondar's crowds, a southern Indian restaurant in Manchester, a hookah cafe in Jinan, or the Senri-Chuo station... The sound is compact and slender, yet it fills a lush basin with the smell of the soil, the smell of the river, it spreads. The feel of rope is alive in both hands, flesh lean from hitting the bell hard.

My grandmother told me a story about my great grandfather when I was young. He was a warm monk who was loved by everyone. Great grandfather's older brother, who should have been in the line of succession of the temple, died in the Russo-Japanese War. They say that he poked his face up from the trench and was shot in the head. At his brother's funeral ceremony, he said that the thought of his deceased brother made him cry. Great grandfather, the successor in the temple, put on a worn robe, traveled on foot and read the sutras of that area, *Ojōhan*. On his return he stopped and drank pure water from the valley river and walked on to the next village.

Occasionally memorial services are prolonged until late at night. Once when great grandfather returned home he came with an animal he called a '*yama*' (literally mountain). This yama was a bit larger than a dog. It had a scar from its mouth to the base of its ear that made it look like some terrible monster. Eventually the wild yama became gentle and affectionate toward great grandfather and sometimes came into the house. When great grandfather pronounced 'yama' he placed a heavy emphasis on the 'ya'—we never knew whether the yama was a variety of wild dog or a wolf.

My grandmother who told me the yama story is now bedridden and lives in nursing home facility. She hardly even recognizes my father, her eldest son. Her close friend still lives in the neighborhood and although elderly she still often works in the fields. I asked her about the yama story and she said she knew nothing of it. The mountain that great grandfather would have seen as he walked to the next village is a gravel mining operation for a concrete factory. The landscape is now so ravaged that the aged mountain too is in pain and exhausted— and the distant howl of the yama still resonates in my heart.

There is only one old, poor-quality photo of great grandfather. It is a commemorative photo of the temple bell going to the army and the war effort in the Pacific. Along with the bell, you can see that the Buddhist fixtures from the main hall were also provisioned. All the gold of the temple would have been offered up for the Pacific War. There are two monks in front of the bell. One is great grandfather and the other is a monk from a nearby temple. This exalted monk in perfectly fitted splendid vestments is next to my stooping great grandfather in his crumpled ragged robes with faded, lack-luster distantly focused eyes. Great grandfather's zest for life had also grown thin. A few years before the war ended, he suddenly collapsed and died. That photo of him was when he was in one of his last years. Behind the bell are about 50 villagers in close quarters for the photo. In my childhood I was familiar with those villagers, who now form a great contrast to the youthful figures in the photograph—indeed many years have gone by.

A woman in the old photo of great grandfather and the bell was grandmother's childhood friend. When she was in elementary school she often went to that friend's house. Grandmother was born in the Meiji era and was called Yō san, one evening she told me that I was a temple boy. I would hear the sound of the bell and bow every night. I would close my eyes, bow, fold my hands in prayer and give thanks in the direction of the sound. I remember that an old woman with deep wrinkles sculpted on her face, praying in this way and thinking that her prayers were granted.

I wonder if the bell was melted for munitions, weapons for soldiers when they traveled so far from their basin homes and crossed oceans to kill others. After the Pacific War a new bell was cast and brought to the temple. I hope the bell that I hit and hit, again and again, and accompanied me as I prayed the Infinite Life Sutra (Muryōjukyō) had a different fate than the one that eventually became munitions.

Prayer 2

There are two things I learned from Elbore James when I was a student and to some degree his understudy in Vancouver. One is that you should not put a beer on the guitar amplifier. The other is that there is no need to have a complicated or even a gentle guitar solo, simply provide accompaniment to songs. Nevertheless, I spent more time going around to clubs with my guitar and participating in jam sessions with other musicians, playing blues scales and solos and endless three chord progressions rather than taking in the lectures at the university. I had great interest in playing and I hung out on the streets for hours at a time. I didn't hang out on a street like Robson Street with its lively scene. I was more comfortable on streets where junkies with guilty looks in their eyes, and drunks hung out, or streets with the brutal feel of some *noire* movie—at such places I felt at home. Daily on my wanderings I would pop into a café on a whim to kill time and listen to cassette tapes that could be had for five Canadian dollars.

On South Marine Drive a rundown bar by the name of Hippos opened the stage to amateur musicians several days a week. Elbore James was one of Hippos' signboard musicians and acted as coordinator for the musicians who came to the bar. The kind of music that is played in Hippos is old blues and rock and roll that flowed into virtually all popular music in the 1960s, but music has moved on since. The name Elbore James is only one letter different than the famous Mississippi slide guitar player, Elmore James. When Elbore takes the stage, he wears a sequin 'Liberace jacket' draped on his shoulders. He jumps, shouts, and seems a bit enamored of himself. He sings rock and roll standards in falsetto. The performance of this middle-aged rock-and-roller with a 1950s Elvis hairstyle full of pomade, is fun, funny, strange, and a bit pathetic. He does the whole act with a dead serious look on his face. He's got all the old moves, hunches over, switching his hands back and forth on his knees which move in knock-kneed and out bowlegged. These old, worn out moves you would never call cool even if you intended to flatter. The drummer was a skillful, middle-aged, mixed-race, indigenous man. When my turn would come, I would crank the volume way up on the amplifier and finger pick the guitar. Even if I was among the better performers taking the stage, I would sometimes mess up a bit and get heckled by the audience, and somebody would quickly turn the sound down. I would persevere long enough to do several old blues songs, but Hippos' was a tough crowd to me and no one listened to my performance. When I would get off the stage only Elbore would praise me saying things like, 'You were good today'—just lip service of course. Elbore, however, always gave me accurate advice on my performances. He warned me off egotistical balls-out solos and encouraged me to play songs like Jimmy Reed. 'Play accurate rhythm as the backbone of the song, the framework. Furthermore, solos are not necessary, and if there is a solo performance it only comes off when the rhythmic backing is solid and extended'.

When you play at Hippos, everyone gets a glass of draft beer for participating in the performances. At one point, I put my beer on the guitar amp. When I picked it up to drink it, I spilled not more than a few drops on the amplifier. Elbore was furious at my carelessness and scolded me, 'Don't put beers on the equipment, you're just going to fuck something up'. I guess it's a natural thing to say. But that's a bitter memory for me from a time when I didn't fully appreciate the goodness of beer.

At one point a giant black singer based in Chicago came to Hippos to sing. As per usual when I hadn't even played yet, he grabbed me as I got off the stage and asked: 'Why do yellow people like you play black music and talk about the blacks' suffering when they were growing cotton'. I couldn't say anything. I just got up and left. After that, he gave an incomparable mind-blowing performance. If I were asked the same thing now, I wonder how I would answer his question.

At dusk when I would soon be returning to Japan, Elbore visited my dorm room to say goodbye. This time he wore a completely different expression that I never saw at Hippos. He said he hadn't had a meal that day and asked me to lend him a little money. He was completely different from the guy at the open stage. He left me feeling lonely because of his timidity and feelings of instability. I never knew his real name only Elbore and he never heard from me again. I hope that he is shouting out good, outdated rock-and-roll in a club and doing his strange routine. Elbore was a hero to me. I want to tell him that if he has a day to meet, I would like to meet him again.

Prayer 3

A singing voice like Tilahun's casts a spell from memories and pulls me back to the streets of Gondar. The singing voice begins to swell with the various sounds of the street: the sound of a whistle played by a beggar; the chant of the bishop of the Ethiopia Orthodox Church; the shouts of the shoe polishers and others hustling customers; the engines of mini-buses and three-wheeled vehicles, the transportation mode of choice in the town. These sounds or in some cases the movement or expression of a specific individual, bring an image of the place, of specific activities, of the smells and humidity—they all come flooding back to my mind and blend with Tilahun's singing voice which spreads out as if a colorful tattoo that is minced in the city's dry, dusty air. I am lying about on my bed in the Ethiopia Hotel at the center of Gondar as per usual. It is a hotel that was built in the late 1930s when the Italian army was stationed here. All the sounds of the streets and its crowds outside are transmitted easily through the thin walls of the building, and the sensation seems to originate from a part of my own body. The miscellaneous sounds mix in me, encroach upon me.

Mohamed is a quiet young man who works at the reception desk of the Ethiopia Hotel. He leans out a window of the second floor, holds a small radio to his ear, looks at the people coming and going on the street below, and occasionally prays to Mecca in one corner of the small reception area. Similarly when I lean out of the window of my room and our eyes meet, a smile comes to my face and I immediately, self-consciously retract my head. Mohamed's fiancé, Bethlehem, has the nickname 'Betty'. In contrast to him, she is jovial, corpulent and impressive with her dimples, a pure young woman. In the evenings, Betty comes to Mohamed's workplace to pick him up. They hold hands and walk back and forth on the street, nothing more. The old capital of Gondar has a majority population that belong to the Ethiopia Orthodox Church. Muslims comprise less than 20% of the population. Romances between couples of a mixed religious devotion in small towns create somewhat of a buzz, a topic of gossip or conversation. In Gondar, the marriage between different religions is not strange yet cannot be said to be common either.

I occasionally raise the topic of trouble stemming from the disparities between religious observances and culinary taboos when members of different religions dine together. Amharic has a euphemistic architectural metaphor describing the marriage between different religious groups or professional communities 'there is a crack in the house'—

an indication that it may not be advisable. Sometimes I meddle and ask Betty and Mohamed if they have difficulties in their everyday life. Relatives on both sides of the families of the two don't think that marriage is a good idea. Betty doesn't intend to convert but is trying to understand Mohammed. Ethiopia's national pop singer, Teddy Afro, hummed a hit song that referenced the romance of lovers from different religions. He smiled at me and indicated with his song:

'It may be a simple structure/ but here is a free house/ swearing enough love for two people/ you have your religion, I have my religion/ I have my religion/ Let's live together'.

One day Betty came to pick up her fiancé at reception and talked to me with a smile as usual. The next morning, she heads to Sudan over land with Mohamed, and they eventually aim for Europe. It seems that Mohammed has relatives in Sudan, but they don't really have fixed plans for the trip. Mohamed remains silent as usual. Tranquil Mohamed and Betty bright as the sun, each one with their eyes on me. I wonder what kind of future their eyes see.

The chant of the Ethiopia Orthodox Church resonates across the Ethiopian Highlands in the twilight. From the Mosque the call to morning prayer echoes out repeatedly from cracked and crackling speakers. The sounds overlap, separate and intersect. I offer my prayer, an addition to that mysterious symphony for the happiness of those two on their journey.

Mischief of the Gods

8

The Promised Land

An apparition on the road appears in the shape of a human but may just be a mass of darkness, the entrance to an infinite otherworld. In a black knit hat and thick black clothes, he carries a big black bag. Tasfay walks over to us while in his bag he collects roadside garbage.

When he appears in the bustling center of Gondar time seems to stop—a jet-black old man in the hustle and bustle of squalid streets. In contrast to his eccentric clothing, he has a soft and gentlemanly demeanor. Tasfay walks away stealthily. He finds me and stops, his soot covered face contorted in a fearless grin. 'Kawase, haven't seen you in a while. How have you been?' His big eyes stare. Tasfay speaks slowly in a sonorous powerful voice. He repeats 'Enen, Enen, Enen, Enen', making a fist with his right hand and hitting his left chest repeatedly. In words it means 'I share your hardships and misfortunes'. *Enen* (me) demonstrates his solidarity and empathy with others. A little old-fashioned but an important physical greeting in northern Ethiopia. When I said, 'Last week, when I went to do research in the countryside, I was bit by fleas and am itchy all over' he repeats, or if someone were to say something like 'Yeah, it's been really cold these days', he comes back with 'Enen, Enen, Enen, Enen'; if you stumble and fall, 'Enen, Enen, Enen, Enen'. Well that's how it is. I liked his gestures and words and while I was trying to imitate them, before I knew it, 'Enen, Enen, Enen, Enen' had become a habit of mine, too. If you do this in the capital or any other big city, everyone will burst out in laughter and ask you where and when you learned such a rustic expression.

A casual chat with Tasfay lifts my spirits. 'Instead of standing out in the open like this', I suggest, 'we should go to a nearby café and have some tea or coffee'. Then Tasfay suddenly becomes displeased, curtly declines my invitation saying 'it's not necessary' and leaves.

A group with an evil eye—that's what has been said of the people of Beta Israel. Beta Israel are the Jews living in Ethiopia. Tasfay was also born Beta Israel in northern Ethiopia. There used to be many settlements of this group in Gondar and its suburbs. While the Beta Israelis are valued by policy makers as a group of professionals, such as pot makers and carpenters, they have been persecuted as a minority in the local community largely due to the pervasive influence of the Ethiopian Orthodox Church. 'A person who is pierced by the evil eye of Beta Israel will die or become ill. Beta Israelis transform into hyenas at night'. Such rumormongering extends from the local people's discriminatory gaze upon this group, and is a clear expression of their feelings, and fear of ethic minority groups.

Since the 1980s there have been several 'rescue' operations conducted under the auspices of the Israeli Law of Return. The majority of Beta Israelis migrated from Ethiopia to Israel. However social discrimination in Israel against Ethiopian Jews, who have long practiced their own doctrines persists, and the group's arduous journey has not come to an end. Tasfay also emigrated to Israel once under an Israeli operation. However, after about ten years, he eventually returned to Gondar, abandoned his faith, and began living in the streets.

A jet-black mass tries to slip by again. I wonder what's up. When I look into Tasfay's gentle, clear eyes, I feel a sense of relief at a long-awaited reunion. He speaks to me in his sonorous voice, saying, 'Enen, Enen'. Tasfay was an English teacher at a southern Ethiopian school when he was young. Things he saw, heard and experienced near his assigned school included two neighboring ethnic groups at war with each other. Two young men elected to settle the disputes between the two groups with a duel. They faced each other armed with spears. A circle of onlookers held its breath, in the next moment the two young men both stabbed one another in the abdomen. They bled profusely and fell to the ground. It is said that the dispute between the two groups was resolved by these deaths. Really? How can that be true—it's more likely that the spears changed nothing. There's a swirl of stories about Tasfay but when it comes to the subject of Israel, where he has spent some years of his life, his demeanor changes and he becomes aloof. 'What kind of place was it? Neither good nor bad. What did you do there? Come on'. 'I forgot all about it'.

Street thugs say Tasfay burns tires and alternately breathes in the smoke and soot through his mouth and then his nose. This act is said to have the effect of diluting the power of his own 'evil eye'. They say that his clothes are all black because tire soot has accumulated on them. Furthermore, it is said that Tasfay can sneak into people's dreams and he gives life improvement advice, and they also say he can predict the future, such as the diseases people will suffer from. I once asked Tasfay about those silly rumors. He reacted neither with anger nor with denial. He nodded slowly with a fearless smile as if everything were factual. I felt dumbfounded, tricked by a fox, no, tricked by his pitch black dark mass. But at the same time, I felt enveloped in an infinitely warm, soft and comfortable darkness and unconsciously a smile spread across my face.

Beta Israel was not the only group that left Gondar. Recently, there has been a sharp increase in the number of young people heading to the Middle East and Europe via Sudan. They pass through the border town of Metemma, which is eight hours northwest of Gondar by bus. In addition, the U.S. Congress started a diversified immigrant visas lottery wherein people could win a visa for the U.S. The number of people who applied increased and the pattern has been that the relatives left in Ethiopia eventually follow relatives who emigrated. In the midst of this, those who once left and 'saw the world', sometimes returned here with shattered dreams, and they rushed out into the streets as if being sucked back into them.

The other groups that left Gondar may be in different situations than Beta Israel, but they leave excited about their new life. Perhaps feeling a sense of superiority with the wind at their backs, feeling that they were finally able to escape. Their peers must have looked at them with envy as they left, too. Yet, after living abroad for several years, if you look into the faces of those who returned, their minds and bodies are like tattered pieces of cloth—they reemerge on the street one after the other.

One example is Fanta, the oldest unofficial tour guide who clings to tourists like a vine, and another is Taye, a tall, thin man who speaks strangely fluent English with a Southern U.S. accent. Both were invited by relatives who had emigrated to the United States, lived there for several years, and eventually returned to Gondar. They spend the day hanging out in the streets, it's a real pain if you get caught by them. All they do is badmouth good people. Their situation must be tough and they probably never have enough food. They are two middle-aged men who look like overripe vegetables. But they aren't bad people. I can't dislike those two guys. I go along with their idle talk. It certainly doesn't look like they're clever, begging for money from tourists, and I have no idea how they get enough to eat. It seems that Fanta has a wealthy brother in the United States who frequently sends him money.

The fate of a young man named Endeshaw is very sad. There was also a young man of about the same age named Bewket. Both Endeshaw and Bewket were inquisitive, intelligent, quick, young men. When they got home from school, they hit the streets. They were fast to approach foreign tourists, attract their attention, and befriend them. In this way, they guided people around the city and earned a small amount of money. It must have been natural for the street guides of the same generation to be jealous of the two. Endeshaw fell in love with an American tourist he met on the street. Before long, the two had a big wedding in Gondar and moved to the United States. The frenzy of the Endeshaw wedding lasted several days. They served delicious mutton that melted in mead. I will never forget the wonderful taste of the food and drink. But then, with astonishing speed, he left the woman and flew back to Gondar. He was soon involved in a car accident in the neighboring town of Maksegnit injuring his head. Afterwards, he became depressed and hanged himself. The incident was so depressing.

Bewket connected with an Australian tourist he met on the streets. The tourist arranged for him to study at a university in Sydney on a scholarship. After studying at the university for two years, he somehow became depressed and eventually ended up going back to Gondar. They say he forgot the names and faces of his old friends on the street and even forgot his own name. From then on he wandered the streets doing nothing but swearing at everyone, picking fights and getting beat up. His face was always covered in cuts and scars. People say he lost his soul and became a fidgety wanderer, a *Qolebiss* (broken spirit).

The street's heat and devilish cold—upon return one is warmly welcome back with open arms as if to say that this is the place you will always return to. In an instant the street throws people away coldly and harshly. Evening dew wets the bodies of those who are thrown away. The night dew sinks to the depths of their hearts and eventually reaches the depths of the dreams they once envisioned. Then the dream solidifies and becomes an ice flower that blooms deep in the heart. What the hell kind of capital is this anyway?

Don't hold anything in your hand
Any memory is in the soul

A silver coin to hell
Even if I hold it in my hand

When you open your hand
Nothing will fall out

Can't be stolen by Atropos
What kind of throne will I bestow upon you

Not withered by the judgment of Minos
What kind of laurel is there

I won't turn you into a shadow
What time do you have

When you arrive at your final destination at night
You will be a shadow

Pick a flower, but throw it away
When I looked at her, she immediately fell out of my hand

Sit in the sun abandon the throne
Then you'll be your own king [2]

Every evening at exactly 6:00 pm in the center of the city a strange ceremony begins, conducted by a strange old man dressed in black. On the streets at the center of Gondar, Tasfay looks up at the evening sky, freezes, he is still as if petrified. No one in particular stops to look at Tasfay or shows particular attention or concern. Around him a distinct calm arises from a corner of the bustling, busy street. Neither the townspeople nor I know ... is it a prayer ... to something or someone special ... or a show. All we know is that tomorrow, Tasfay will form a dark mass in the same place at the same time and repeat this ritual.

8

The Promised Land

9

Eternity

I met you in that dark, damp bar up the hill. You were born into a poor family in a rural village in North Gondar. Your father was drafted into the Ethiopian-Eritrean War but did not return, and your mother was sickly and left you in this world as a young child. You were first placed in an aunt's house, but you didn't get along well with her and were sent to another relative's home. You were in your late teens, treated like a servant in every household, never went to school and forced to do hard labor. In the end you escaped to the city of Gondar. Shortly after arriving in town you found a job as a waitress at a small café inside the bus station. You caught on to the job quickly and easily and managed to get by on your own. You stayed in those huts where most tenants were farmers from nearby farms who came to the market.

Through an acquaintance you got a job in a bar as a waitress. You wore tight clothes and went night after night dancing to deafeningly loud pop music that you didn't really like. As you danced in the swirl of sound your heart was never in it. But you didn't nihilistically look down on the crazy men who dance so happily. You made ends meet in musty bars being stared at by men, listening to drunks talk, and selling her body as solicited.

Late at night you leave the bar, shave your pubic hair and put a few rubbers in your pocket and go to a cheap hotel where customers are waiting. Most of the innkeepers are your acquaintances. Even if that wasn't the case, you could tell the front desk clerk with a friendly smile that you were invited by a guest and you could go straight to the room. If by any chance you were about to be kicked out of the hotel, all you'd have to do is hand the person at the desk a tip.

You had many kinds of customers: some sadistic guys who got agitated by your stubborn refusal and reluctance, some with tendencies that seemed almost insane, some even fled without paying. Still you accepted countless kisses and hugs from men. You kill yourself over and over again, discarding your body in the darkness of night. You are shattered and scattered in the cold nights of Gondar. After 'the act' you grab a glass bottle full of water in your left hand, pullout a bedpan kept under the bed, squat down on it and use the water to quickly wash your genitals with your right hand. After that you leave your hotel room without even lying on the bed. You happen to be uncircumcised and that sometimes attracts the worship of customers—the owner of a clitoris, a highly sensitive protrusion, known as a 'rose antenna'. For the customers who turn their attention to the protrusion with curiosity, you jokingly let them think that you are from the Qimant ethnic group of Gondar who don't practice female circumcision.

Many women have drifted to the bar to work. They come to Gondar from all over and become your friends. They all wear gaudy make-up, smell like cheap soap, and cast shadows like thick, heavy curtains. They didn't all come to Gondar to become bar girls, nor were they all driven into poverty, many choose this job. Some lost their parents and had nowhere to return to; some longed for city life; some came looking for educational opportunities; some fought with their families and left home; and some drifted away looking to find relatives.

Many guests bring rubbers but don't at all want to use them. Some of your co-workers suffer from diseases that are likened to 'the joker', the trump card. You took care with all your heart until the very end of orphaned women who were reduced to skin and bones because of the misfortunes of that disease. Your colleague and best friend Salam was one of them. Salam used to be a dancer in traditional music clubs in the capital's hotels and restaurants. According to Salam, Gondar's patrons are much quieter and better off than those of the *Chechenia*, 'streets of the immoral' in Addis Ababa. At those bars you could get tangled up with drunken customers and meet with a bad end. One time Salam yelled at a customer, she was protective of you—it was one of her roles to kick out such troublemakers from the bars. Men would be overwhelmed and wither in the face of her threats and anger. In the end the powerful Salam was killed by the joker. It is said that Salam has two young children who beg in the streets of Addis Ababa.

In an extremely dark bar women with languid expressions seem to float in cheap, flashy neon lighting. Your co-workers are little more than background paintings to you. They make you stand out. You are unlike other women, you laugh and talk a lot. You are very bright and charming. Most of the guys who come to the bar are obviously looking for you. But many of the men who want you aren't good people. There are a few who look decent. But what is decent? Your hope is to have a long-term, stable relationship with someone of good pedigree, or at least someone who at first seems decent and to have some money. You often invite the men you like to your house during the day and treat them to a feast of chili-stewed chicken, *doro wat*, and fragrant coffee. The sharp hearts of many men are softened by this and next, you take the men's dirty clothes and wash them. The men's hearts begin to melt like butter.

Various men have passed in front of your eyes: soldiers guarding the border, tanker truck drivers transporting oil from Sudan, Chinese road workers, Italian backpackers, American aid workers, but all quickly disappear after promising to take you abroad. You put the men's portraits and photos that you received as souvenirs in a small album tucked away in a drawer. One day you fell in love with Zelalem, a young man whose name means 'eternity' in Amharic. He was a rare, taciturn and straight-laced man and maybe that's a given because you didn't meet him at the bar.

Zelalem loved you. He knew of your profession and didn't want you to go to the bar in the evenings with your makeup and your head full of cheap Middle Eastern perfume. He hated your tight jeans. There were guys in your past who half tried to force you out of working at bars. But you have rent to pay, you need the ingredients for cooking meals, and coffee beans for coffee ceremonies, your socializing with neighbors. You can't quit the bar so easily. When really short on money, you whisper to men in bed and get many times the normal amount of tips. However you know from experience that men won't last long—they always prove unreliable.

But you quit the bar without a second thought to be together with Zelalem. Your female co-workers were both surprised and delighted to hear that you had finally met a decent man. You helped run a small general store with Zelalem. Soap, cooking oil, tissue paper, biscuits and water constitute little more than the selection of goods sold by street vendor children. However, little by little the number of items increased as did the number of customers coming to the general store. You were happy. One day Zelalem found your precious little album hidden in the corner of your room. The eyes of the men who sought you in the past silently stared at him. He punched and kicked you, shred all your photographs and scattered them around the room. You had a nosebleed, sat trembling in the corner of the room crying. But Zelalem was the only person you wanted to devote your life to and you were the only object of his quiet, intense passion. Eventually you gave birth to a boy who looked just like Zelalem. Then as if none of this had happened, he left you and moved to some other town. Life was hard for you with a toddler, 'lij aschegari naw' it's hard to raise a child. Former female colleagues at the bar as well as the neighbors who used to be close to you assumed that you were financially supported by male patrons, and did not give you a hand. One day you heard a rumor on the wind that Zelalem died in a distant city. You stood once again in the dim, damp bar on that hill.

9

Eternity

9

Eternity

10

Mischief of the Gods

Great Serpent of the Wasteland Dereb, come here
Great Serpent of the Wasteland Dereb, hurry up and come here

The fragrant smoke of roasting coffee beans and burner coals together fills the room with white cloud. On a stringed masenqo the Azmari boy Tigabu sings a monotonous melody to summon the spirit *Dereb*. There are many *qole* (spirits in Amharic). The qole have names, hometowns, and a variety of personalities. *Bule* of the wasteland, *Shankit*, the black slave, Sofi the Muslim, *Seifuchangir* the whip, and the serpent Dereb are just a few. They are all formidable with no chinks in their armor; they are mischievous and whimsical, they protect people, deceive them, and kill them. Dereb is a ferocious god who comes from the wastelands of north Gondar with many soldiers in tow behind him. On one occasion a couple in their mid-thirties sit in consultation in front of a medium: 'I have been married for nine years but have no children. Tonight, I'm going to ask the serpent Dereb of the wasteland to gift me a child'. The medium Abeba is a *feress* (horse).

The medium Abeba is the sister of the farmer I stay with. She is quiet and kind, and frequently visits her father. Abeba lives with her husband and three children about fifty meters downhill from the farmhouse where I stay. She took the trouble to stop by Solomon's house to see if I was doing well and adapting to the unfamiliar farm life. The night sky of the Ethiopian Highlands in the dry season is filled with countless stars. One day, when I said that I wanted to sleep outdoors in a sleeping bag gazing at the stars, Abeba's father Solomon, who was the head of the family, strongly opposed this saying that I would be eaten by hyenas. There was a plausible tale in that farming village that if someone went out alone after eight o'clock at night, he would be attacked by a pack of hyenas. According to Solomon the caretaker next door was eaten by hyenas, they left only his wrists. I don't know if this is Solomon's exaggeration in an attempt to frighten me or if it's a true story. In any case, Abeba persuaded her father, and in the end Solomon was going to sleep next to me out in the open with a Kalashnikov.

I discovered the 'possession ritual' called 'zar' because shortly after going to bed one night I heard a ruckus in the direction of Abeba's house. People could be heard cheering and clapping along with what sounded like a *taiko* drum keeping a gentle beat. I immediately got up to rush over and see what was going on. Then the children of the house, Solomon and Solomon's wife got up and forcefully stopped me from going over there. 'Is there a wedding party in the middle of the night like this? What the hell is going on?' Even when I asked everyone just looked at me awkwardly and wouldn't explain what was going on. This family's demeanor piqued my curiosity even more and made me want all the more to know what was going on down the hill. Breaking free from Solomon and his family, I descended the rolling hills and visited

Abeba's house. Looking through the partially open door, I saw about thirty people squatting on the dirt floor with their knees in their arms, clapping their hands and wearing solemn expressions. A few people were drumming plastic oil jugs as improvised drums. And at the center of the group is Abeba. She opens her eyes and spreads her arms wide. She flutters her arms like she's a bird stuck in a swamp desperately trying to fly. She's yelling into the void. The calm, composed person I know is not present. I was a little shocked by her ferocious expression and her behavior, yet I joined the group.

It is said that Abeba once suffered some physical distress that included pain in the limbs, some discomfort when drunk, feeling that something like a cloth was covering her eyes, and a sensation like her back was covered. She was bedridden for months. Subsequently she began having dreams every night in which she would mate with a serpent. Once her dreams of sex with the serpent began, she had little sexual contact with her husband. In the meantime, a ritual called zar was held night after night and many qole were summoned to Abeba. As a result, relatives and neighbors began coming to consult the spirits who had come to Abeba. Since that time Abeba has been consulted about all sorts of problems, such as, marital quarrels, daughter-in-law disputes, a son's drinking habit, searching for lost items, and a daughter's advancement to higher education.

A performance by Azmari musicians is indispensable at a zar. An Azmari plays and sings the stringed masenqo to the cues of the medium. Thus, Azmaris play the role of calling qole to the medium. Among them, there are some Azmaris who not only perform but also translate the qole's somewhat indecipherable expressions so that the participants can easily understand them. With my help the young Azmari Tigabu was invited to perform whenever a zar was held by Abeba. Azmaris who perform at zars are paid in advance by the mediums. The pay is enough for Tigabu to cover a few weeks cost of living in the city. Standards for payment at wedding banquets or bar shows are financially ambiguous activities, however by comparison, the rewards for zar performances are quite good. I know that Tigabu doesn't really like zar performances because sometimes one is required to play all night long, and the qole can be capricious and violent. Such qole are called *ronqe* in Azmari jargon. Most Azmaris hate zar as it is generally regarded as heresy. The Ethiopian Orthodox Church views zar as a demonic possession that misleads people. The church severely criticizes those who practice it. The Monk Birhanu, who I am familiar with in the city, admonished me to stay away from zars and told me about their origins.

The story of God creating twelve angels goes like this: suddenly the world was covered with darkness and the angels were very uneasy. Among the twelve angels was an angel named Diablos. He said to the other angels, 'I am the one who created you, follow me'. The other angels asked, 'If you are really the Creator, create man too prove it to us'. Diablos was able to deftly create human bodies one after another, however, they lacked souls. Some angels didn't believe Diablos at all, but some were at a loss as to whether what Diablos said was true or not. At that point Saint Gabriel appeared. He advised the angels, 'Worship with all your heart and face the true God, even if it's just for a day'. When the angels did so suddenly God appeared. Diablos, who was sitting on a golden throne tumbled into darkness the moment God appeared. After that, Diablos began to perform the zar, and the descendants of Diablos inherited this ritual and conducted it from generation to generation.[3]

The monk continues his explanation, 'However, if you drink the *tsabal* (holy water) of the church, the medium will stop the zar'.

Zar is held on festivals related to the Ethiopian Orthodox Church and on festivals such as New Year. If you don't think about it too much, it's an odd and curious story. The Orthodox Church thoroughly denies zar and hates the practice. According to Tigabu, Azmaris gather and feast on these festival days too. Also connected to the festivals, people sing and dance energetically. It is said that the smells, sounds, and bustling of people and the heat generated by all this wakes up the sleeping creatures in wastelands and lakes far away and beckons them to where ritual's taking place.

Abeba wraps a white cloth around her head, sits down on the floor, looks up in the sky, mutters something and slowly sways her upper body back and forth in time with Tigabu's music. In order to welcome the qole, she must be well prepared. People spread grass all over the floor, place sheep's liver (said to be the qoles' favorite) around the floor, and carefully prepare the space for the ritual. Qole loves the blood and meat of animals, and it is said that qole tilts its head and sips the blood that drips to the ground when sheep and chickens are sacrificed. Qole also like a variety of scents: incense, the aroma of roasting coffee, and perfumes (especially imported varieties), these scents are necessities for a zar. Alcoholic beverages are also essential. A distilled liquor called *araqe* is often served to participants during rituals. Tigabu tells me never to drink this alcoholic liquor because when I drink hard liquor, I often fall asleep. Tigabu uses different melodies and lyrics according to the characteristics and tastes of each qole. And he sometimes improvises creating lyrics to attract and entertain them.

Zar participants are called *amuamuaki* (warmers) or *ankeskash* (shake to wake from sleep). The smells, sounds, bustle and heat generated in the space with everyone gathered including others invited from far away attract the qole. When the energy and heat is inadequate or half-hearted, the qole become furious, 'ride' the horse (the medium) wildly, and the qoles rage eating young black olive leaves and dancing in the fire. It is said that all this not only makes the medium sick, but also brings misfortune to those involved in the ritual.

Something is wrong. Maybe it's because I'm shooting film, or maybe it's because of the camera light, but it takes a long time for Abeba to transform into a horse.

God, you got everything you wanted
Our god, come down
Come on God, you've got everything you wanted
God of North Gondar, come down

The god here does not represent the God of the Christian Orthodox Church. Abeba points at qole. In zar the distinction between Christian God and qole is blurred—the boundary dissolves; Muslims participate; monks from churches that deny zar during the day, sometimes participate.

Seven or eight people form a circle and clap their hands to the music of Tigabu. Suddenly, Abeba dances into the center of the room her hair is disheveled and she begins to spin violently. With this movement as a signal, everyone forces out a joyful cry from the depths of their throats: 'Iruruururururu'. It is the signal that Dereb has arrived. The masenqo melody that Tigabu repeats is powerfully accelerated. At that moment, a chill runs through my body, I start to have spasms, and I seem to have lost control of my body, it won't move as I want. I put down my camera, lay down on the dirt floor, and watch the ceremony. As Tigabu plays, he glances anxiously at me. The playing stops.

Abeba's face lit by the candlelight is grim and painfully contorted. Abeba's eyes pierce a woman participant. Then a man summons the woman his wife, to his side. He suddenly and violently stripped her of her clothes and undergarments. Abeba immediately and violently squirts the araqe in her mouth and on her breasts. My body doesn't move. I feel nauseous.

Tigabu picks up the masenqo and starts playing again. Now Abeba hurls lyrics at Tigabu. Actually, at this point Dereb speaks through Abeba, and she has become the horse that the qole rides. Tigabu repeats the words that come out of Abeba's mouth word for word, and sets them to a melody on the masenqo.

Leaving the northern wasteland and wandering around
I found this woman (Abeba)
You don't have enough incense or coffee beans
Aren't you afraid of me?

Abeba, or rather, Abeba's body, utters fragmentary and incoherent words, sometimes screams, shakes its head violently from side to side, turns its upper body, and continues to rock back and forth. The great serpent of the wasteland, Dereb, is wild riding Abeba, the horse, singing and dancing like an idiot and toying with others gathered there. Lying on the dirt floor and holding back my nausea, I stare at the events before me.

It seems that the couple decided on the date of the next ceremony and exchanged a *silat* (promise of tribute) to qole, which will be prepared by that date. After a while Abeba lowered her head and she crouched down. A dead silence reigns over this room in the farmhouse. Dereb has apparently returned to his wilderness lair in North Gondar. The space after the qole has left is said to be 'cold'. Then, as if the spell has lifted, the agony and sickness I was feeling left me. I wonder what has happened. I sit up and move to sit down beside Tigabu. Abeba has regained her usual gentle and soft expression, and she is worried about me, wondering if Kawase is okay.

Even though I've been to many zar ceremonies, I've never experienced such an inexplicable change in my body as this time. It could have been food poisoning or a mild cold or it could have been a prank by the serpent Dereb. Tigabu grinned and said, he just liked the qole. I'll play the masenqo and sing whenever the Kawase starts the next zar.

Unfortunately, we have not heard of that couple ever having children.

10

Mischief of the Gods

11

Mischief of the Gods

Qolo Temari

Gebre prays at the eaves of private houses repeating, 'Sele egzihabher' (I am begging in the name of God). The pimply-faced mid-teenage boy is a proselytizer of the Ethiopian Orthodox Christian Church: a qolo temari. He travels in a hemispherical hat made of sheep's fur and a cotton cloak that covers the whole body, he carries a freshly tanned cowhide pochette that holds a small Bible and a wooden cane to ward off stray dogs.

Novice clergy are called qolo temari: 'qolo' is a light meal made of roasted barley, which is a snack to go with coffee or alcoholic drinks; 'temari' in this case refers to those who learn the teachings of the church. Poor or wealthy, no matter the economic situation, qolo is the only thing on the table at home. Qolo is the minimum reward from the people that a qolo temari gives prayers and words of blessings to. Gebre receives exclusively injera. Most of it is leftover food that doesn't retain its original shape, especially the injera that's been baked for a few days and is dry. It sometimes gives off a musty, unpleasant odor. Some houses will give money to Gebre, but only on limited occasions such as around big festivals or at the New Year.

'Brother, how are you?' 'Thank God I am fine' (Efo WeAlke Egziabhere Yisebah) it goes in Amharic. Amharic is the commonly used language, Ethiopia's official language, and it has its roots in *Geez*. The Geez language is used in the Bible and on ceremonial occasions. When Gebre learns new words and phrases in Geez, he tries them out before he fully comprehends the content of those words. Care must be taken in the occasions and timing. Practicing the newly learned Geez language on an elderly clergyman can lead to misuse and be quite embarrassing. Gebre was born in a farming village at the foot of the Ras Dashen Mountains. At the behest of his devout farmer parents, he was placed in a church in the city of Gondar. Gebre himself had no clear idea of what it meant to join the Church, but he certainly wanted to experience something more than rural life. He had also seen since childhood that the clergy who frequented the countryside were respected by the people, and he vaguely thought that the work was probably not bad. He belongs to the Ba'eta Church. It is a church dedicated to the Virgin Mary, an important pillar of the Orthodox faith. He was constantly taught by his parents that Ethiopia was a gift from God to the Virgin Mary. This church is renown as a place of severe training for qolo temari. A few people who joined the clergy at the same time as Gebre have run away.

Orthodox believers are usually required to observe periods of fasting called tsom. Tsom days are Wednesdays and Fridays each week. In addition, there are six short-term and long-term official periods of fasting and the Ethiopian Orthodox Church requires its followers to observe a total of about 180 tsoms a year. Naturally, clergy who belong to the church are subject to a stricter and longer tsom. During tsom, people avoid butter, meat, and other animal proteins and switch to a vegetarian diet. Also, they avoid going out for entertainment such as drinking alcoholic beverages, singing and dancing. Gebre and other qolo temaris do not drink anything, let alone eat, from sunrise to

15:00 in the afternoon. The purpose of tsom is to weaken one's body by moderation in one's life and to change one's attitude toward life which in general tends to be self-centered. This teaching is just as in Matthew Chapter 4, 'man does not live by bread alone, but by every word that comes out of the mouth of God'. Among tsom, the most important for clerics, commoners, and any believers is arba tsom. This tsom lasts for a little less than two months. Everyone loses a few kilograms because of the ascetic and strict nature of arba tsom. Arba tsom ends with Fasika, the feast of the resurrection of Christ (Easter). People give earth-shaking cheers as the date changes and they welcome in Fasika. This is Gebre's favorite time of the year. The day after the end of the tsom people eat raw beef and drink mead, teji, and dance to celebrate. Those who have made the mistake of accidentally eating meat during the period of vegetarianism, go to church, repent and ask God's forgiveness.

Heading into the main entrance of the church Gebre belongs to, if you enter the path along the wall on the left, you will see a thatched hut where the qolo temari live. Five or six people live cramped into one hut. From early morning to noon, they go around to private houses and collect people's leftovers. In the afternoon they stay around the hut to read and recite the Bible in Geez. Little by little a novice has to clear exams given by seniors to climb the stairs to become a clergyman. Worship begins when the wooden planks hanging at the entrance of the church are struck. Long, slow, incantation-like prayers are chanted by the priests responsible for the ritual music. They are called *debtera*. Debteras wear a white cloth wrapped around the head. Behind them are high-ranking clerics who wear black cylindrical hats. In the debtera's left hand is a ceremonial staff, and in his right hand is a metal instrument called a *tsinatsel*. They gently rock the tsinatsel left and right to create sound. On the right is a ceremonial drum, a kebero. The act of hitting the ground with the tip of the staff during the ritual represents Jesus being whipped, and the swaying of the tsinatsel and the beat of the kebero represent Jesus Christ being beaten by the crowd and staggering along slowly making his way up the hill of Calvary. Between lengthy ceremonies the clerics rest by leaning against this staff. Gebre falls into a deep drowsiness amidst the repetition of tsinatsel and all the percussion. Orthodox ritual music is called *zema*, and legend has it that it was composed by the sixth-century Saint Jared who was inspired by the voices of birds. Zema is said to be a gift from God and is deeply rooted in Orthodox life.

During his morning activities, Gebre takes off his qolo temari costume, carries food for hotels and restaurants, and also carries materials for houses under construction to earn a little money. Part-time jobs are prohibited by the church. He has to go to an area of some distance so that the other qolo temari won't know about it. On the way he passes a cottage where foreign tourists often stay. One day a ferenje (foreigner) beckoned Gebre. He was offered a seat on the terrace at the entrance of the cottage and had a little Coca-Cola to drink. Gebre's plump cheeks turned red as he drank the lukewarm cola which made him immediately break into a smile. The next time they met, the foreigner offered him a seat and a drink of Sprite. Then one day he was forced to drink beer. He found it bitter and far from a pleasant. However it was alluring enough to help forget the harshness of everyday life for a moment.

At the end of the day when going to bed, life in the countryside resurfaces in Gebre's mind. A farmer's morning comes early. It's not that Gebre misses his days in the farming village. It's been a year since he started living in the hut next to the church although it seems like decades have passed. Gebre, the youngest of six siblings, would rise in the morning from his bed of goat fur on a dirt floor, urged to get up at the crowing of roosters before the sun rises. He has a ragged blanket that covers him from head to toe. With the blanket wrapped around him he steps out into the twilight cold. His mother milks a cow in the pen beside the house. Gebre drinks fresh milk from a well-smoked gourd container. Then he drives the cattle out of the wooden fence up the hill to pasture. A group of farmers heading to the city walks along the highway just below the hill. Some carry canes with chickens dangling upside down over their shoulders, others drive dozens of sheep—all are moving at close to jogging speed. Among the group Gebre's father and brother can be seen hurrying on the road to the city with jute bags

11

Qolo Temari

filled with grain on their backs. When Gebre's father's errands settle down he spends time in the tavern in town. He enjoys drinking mead in the daytime with the farmers more than anything else.

Gebre guards the cows as they graze and throws pebbles just hard enough to not hurt their skin of the ones trying to escape from the herd. Frightened they immediately return to the herd. While keeping an eye on the cows slowly grazing he takes out a bamboo washint flute. A shaky melody echoes across the plateau and out of nowhere, several slightly older shepherds rush up to him. The shepherds bombard him with questions in rapid succession, such as 'what's the groom's name' who Gebre's 14-year-old sister is about to marry in a neighboring village, or 'the number of livestock in the household', but Gebre has no answers. Until the day of the ceremony even the bride does not know what kind of person the groom will be. Gebre keeps playing the washint with his head down. Before long the shepherds begin dancing the *iskista* in a circle as a kind of 'rehearsal' for the wedding. It's a dance in which the shoulders are violently undulated. And they shout out 'Ururururu' in a throttled falsetto. The girls carrying vessels of water on their backs to their homes, put them aside on the road and enter the bustling circle. A generous amount of butter from the girls' hair runs down their foreheads. Gebre's older brother Kiros plows the fields with cows. The oxen draw wooden plows as Kiros holds the handle in his left hand and beats the sky with the whip in his right hand. With the sound of the whip the cows change direction and speed. Gebre admired the way his brother skillfully controlled the oxen and learned by imitating him. At first he was overwhelmed by the power of the oxen and was a poor driver. When he finally learned the basics of the plow and driving the oxen, he began to enjoy controlling them. Then he was sent to the local church.

Bestiality is not uncommon among village youths, but no one has been more involved in having sex with donkeys than Kiros. The petite Kiros cannot reach the donkey's genitals. If stones are piled up and he can climb up to reach them. The donkey is reluctant and tries to run away. Gebre's technique is to wrap the donkey's face in his own jacket and hold him down during the act. Kiros' jacket is made in China and a shoddy piece of clothing but in Kiros' mind it's similar to what Michael Jackson wore. Kiros refers to it as the 'Michael Jackson Jacket' and wears it proudly. One day with the help of Gebre, Kiros tried to have sex with the donkey but that day the donkey taught Kiros a lesson. The donkey slipped away and ran around the village wearing Kiros' pride, the Michael Jackson jacket on his head. The donkey gained a brief moment of freedom and bayed loudly. When the peasants of the village saw the donkey running around in the Michael Jackson jacket, they instantly knew what had happened.

As soon as you step into a Ba'eta Church the smell of fragrant incense fills the air and you are surrounded by colorful icons that dazzle. You can see dust float and rise in the rays of light coming through the windows of the church. An image of Mary holds the infant Jesus, and you see the winged angels Michael and Gabriel who are messengers connecting God and mankind. Gabriel has a dragon underfoot, a 'dirty soul' *Erkus Menfes* is written next to the dragon. Demons and dragons are painted blue and have only one eye—it is said that the moment they have two eyes a terrifyingly evil power will manifest and attack people. 'Was this a trick of the ancient professional painters to draw only one eye instead of two?' For Gebre the numerous paintings in the church are not just paintings that trace the miracles and sufferings of Jesus and the saints, they are actually breathing, living prayers, curses, punishments, and the very embodiment of God's love. Surrounded by the images of these saints, he secretly envisioned himself as a 'father of souls' (*nefse abbat*) who would reach out to the lost and bless them. 'Imagine yourself as such or maybe you can't stand the rigorous training and will instead return to your village in the Ras Dashen Mountains'. However Gebre takes a deep breath and recommits himself to staying a little longer.

12

Mischief of the Gods

A Promise
to Yohannis

When was it? I ran out of Japanese notebooks I brought for my field research, so I purchased some cheap ones in Gondar. I scribbled down lyrical fragments of traditional Amharic songs, but didn't make written records of much else. There were blank spaces, blank pages, Japanese and English research too that had just been tossed aside in a corner. A colleague who visited my lab once dug out some of those notebooks from the garbage piles in my room and started flipping through them. Some crumbled in his hands due to such poor storage. There was yellow discoloration on the edges in some places, while some places were still in good condition. There were partial pages, parts missing, and loose pages not even integral to a notebook. There was scribbling in places where I couldn't make out what was written. While telling the colleague that it was embarrassing and asking him to stop, I picked up one of those notebooks myself. Being careful not to fray it any further I looked more closely at a photograph of a dear friend. I continued turning pages taking great care not to let the pages crumble. Here and there was graffiti left by children that ranged from abstract designs to highly accomplished paintings, to what appear to be practice writing the alphabet. I knew that some children who came in and out of my room at the Ethiopia Hotel made changes and contributions to the notebooks and I didn't particularly blame them for their curiosity. I did not however request that they write in them either. Yet, when I look at it now, I can see that there are so many images inhabiting my notebooks that I can't help but assert myself here and there. In the midst of this a painting with the autograph of a boy named Yohannis stands out. You can see ancient warriors, live-stock, people interacting, dinner tables, and ordinary people attending church. Take for example a picture of a warrior, a colorful warrior with a mustache, holding a sharp sword and a circular shield stomping barefoot on the ground. There was a hairstyle that looks like some kind of graph—it was a braid that ran along the scalp called a 'shurubba' in the local Amharic language and due to its arrangement is thought to represent 'cornrows', precisely the term used in English. It is said that Emperor Theodore II and his warriors who fought valiantly against the British army in the 19th century, wore this hairstyle. It is likely that the picture was drawn in the image of a former brave warrior of Ethiopia. Yohannis' paintings are by no means skilled, they are rather naïve actu-ally. Nonetheless, these paintings constitute subject matter that makes us think about the lifestyle, history, and culture of the local community in northern Ethiopia, and they are of interest for precisely this reason.

Yohannis is the younger brother of a research assistant who has been indebted to me for a long time. Gondar is home to the Simien National Park, which includes World Heritage Archaeological sites and

Mount Ras Dashen, Ethiopia's highest peak. As one of Ethiopia's leading tourist destinations, it is often visited by foreign tourists. After school, Yohannis made it a daily routine to busily run around the city, hustling tourists who came to town, introducing them to hotels and restaurants, and showing them around ruins and churches. In the local Amharic slang, there is a word *arada*, an expression used to describe the shrewd, cunning, and trendy urban youth. Handsome and nimble, Yohannis was a typical arada, so he got along well with girls and made good money. The inquisitive Yohannis and his fellows would often visit me when I came over from Japan and we'd spend time together. In retrospect, these drawings must have been created at that time, and I think that through my interactions with Yohannis, I was able to obtain a lot of information about the manners and customs of young people in Gondar and what happened on the street. When I was leaving to go back to Japan, I remember him silently looking down to hide his tears.

One day, Yohannis fell ill and suddenly lost his eyesight. He spent some time in the biggest hospital in town. He also ordered *tsabal* (holy water) from distant churches to drink, which was said to have great potency. However, he showed no signs of getting better and rapidly weakened. The last time I went to visit him, he held my hand and asked me to buy him a Japanese Walkman and bring it to him. I promised I would bring one with me the next time I came to Gondar. I remember the feeling of Yohannis' ice-cold hand at this time, and the strength of his grip that did not match the cold. Yohannis died shortly afterward and in the end the promise was never fulfilled.

Upon opening the notebook, scribbles that were holding their breath here and there start chatting with each other and spin a story and invite me to the hustle and bustle of the streets of Gondar.

13

Mischief of the Gods

Reacquainted

Upon meeting a former acquaintance, Tigist:

Welcome to Huddersfield, Kawase. It's a nothing town with nothing to do, right? Facebook is amazing. Thank you for finding me, I never dreamed I'd see you again and just like that! And then to find you are living nearby in Cheadle Hulme, England. In England? Yeah I been here about two years, I think. I make fifty pounds a week and have a small accommodation as you can see. I am currently training to become a beautician here. I met my husband in Sudan when traveling from Gondar to Sudan. My child was born here. I can't possibly tell anyone the truth about myself. Who we are and where we come from ... just can't tell people. We say we're asylum seekers from Eritrea. It's easier to get a residence permit than to come out and honestly say we're from Ethiopia. The *balsiltan* (officials) here have no idea about our situation. Huh, did I change? Well, a lot has happened. Getting here was a long and arduous journey. After getting out of Sudan we went to Libya. I don't even want to think about that. The place is full of hair-raising thugs. We were deceived by intermediaries who swiped our money and goods. We were on a midnight crossing on a boat in the Mediterranean Sea that capsized and half of the twenty-four people drowned. My husband's sister too, right in front of us. The feeling I had when I was desperately clinging to the boat and waiting for my life to be saved, I am telling you! Drifting in the ocean for hours. Our skin was sodden—let's stop talking like this.

In Gondar everyone hangs out a lot. I was still a student in my mid-teens when you came to town. Aren't you nostalgic? How many years have passed since then? I heard on the wind that Ephrem died in an accident. Yes, the youngest of the family that ran your hotel. From beggars to Azmari children, the innkeeper hated you for letting just anyone into your room and making a lot of noise. Both the eldest son, the banker, and the second son thought it would be good if you left. Only Ephrem, the youngest, was kind to everyone. He was a really good boy. For such a good young man to die first even the Virgin Mary was little help in this case. How is that Azmari, Tigabu? He was always with you. That kid really had perseverance even when he was abused and slandered, he went about his business calmly.

Is the butcher in Jan Tekele Park still there? I heard he died some time ago. We all went there a lot together, huh? Spring sheep in Wales are delicious, but I'll never forget the taste of the lamb and beef I ate under the giant fig tree in Jan Tekele Park. What about the bar near the park? The mead they served was not as tasty but are people still going there? You haven't changed a bit. How are Johnny, Alex, Nega and the infamous Gondar street guides doing? You used to yell at each other every time you passed each other. As soon as foreign tourists came to town, Kawase, you spread bad rumors about the guides to the tourists and kept the guides away. As a result they had less work to do, but they got enough to eat, right?

Those guys were always angry at you. Remember all those tricks they devised to get money out of the *ferenje* (tourists)? Thinking about it now, it's terrible. They take foreign tourists to *teji bet* (mead taverns) and yebahil mishit bet (traditional music clubs) and demand high referral fees. The worse story is what Arega did. He said that he would take tourists on a trekking tour of Mount Ras Dashen, so he received a deposit, rented a minibus, and passed through Gondar. After about an hour's drive, we arrived at the Tsedda market. Telling the tour guests that they were stopping for a restroom break, they dropped them off at this market, and the guides took off with the car. That ass Arega repeated this trick without learning his lesson. *Zappa* (police) didn't catch me because I'm agile, but I've been accused of being a really bad guide by Lonely Planet and even on the Internet. *Balage* (the worst kind), you know?

You used Amharic to swear at them whenever you learned new words in the streets. I always shed tears of laughter at your cat-and-mouse game. Those kids are already grown up and have office positions, sounds like bullshit but it's true. Huh, did you make up? Alex got a *VISA* (Amharic slang for 'foreign woman') and is in Europe? Baye is still hanging out in the streets. It's just like him. What do you miss about Ethiopia? Do you get asked questions as stupid as that? You know everything about that, don't you? I wonder if someday I will be able to succeed here and return to Gondar. Maybe God only knows. Oh yeah. I bought this *drqqosh* (dried injera) at a market in London. Of course, it's made from *teff* (the grain that's used to make injera). Look, I've made a *doro wat*, so eat it before it gets cold.

Tigist, welcome to Cheadle Hulme. Nice to see you again. I never thought that we would be able to meet like this again. No, I'm surprised because we are both in England, not Gondar or Addis Ababa. It's a little quieter and calmer than the bleak city center of Stockport. What with the graceful call of blackbirds, the tastefully landscaped parks and the posh cafes and restaurants here. It's so different from the back streets of Gondar. I'm taking my daughter to nursery school, but it's all white moms, and they all speak Mancunian English with strong Manchester accents, so I have no idea what they're saying.

Sometimes I miss injera and go to the *Habesha* (Ethiopian) restaurant on Sackville Street in the heart of Manchester. One can feast on *doro wat* (chicken stewed with onions, peppers and boiled eggs) and *yetsom beyaynet* (beans, cabbage, potatoes, beets and other vegetables). But if you're after the real taste of home, *shero wat* (a stew of several types of bean flour), that's quite satisfying. What do you like about injera? What's with asking that kind of question? I'm sure you're into that sour taste. But *gebs injera* (barley mixed injera) is sometimes too sour for my taste. I'm fine with a regular injera with a teff base. But Habesha Restaurant's Ethiopian food is terrible! It has very little teff and is covered with baking and rice powder. It looks nice and tastes fine but there is something different about it. Why does my stomach feel strangely swollen and uncomfortable after eating it? I've never come across decent injera in England, or in any Ethiopian restaurant in Europe for that matter. Of course it's the same in Tokyo and Osaka. Wait, come to think of it, there's one good place in London—a place to get delicious injera. Just between you and me, I often go on business trips to London and when leaving Cheadle Hulme Station, you arrive at Euston Station in 2 hours and 16 minutes at the quickest. After exiting the station, walk along the street with the British Library on your left. Approaching St. Pancras Station my heart begins to throb a little. Yes, behind the station there lies the diagonal Caledonian Road. As you know, there are many Ethiopian restaurants and cafes in that area. There's a hair salon run by Ethiopian staff and a general store. A Habesha presence has just arrived in England. First, go to a restaurant run by Habesha on Caledonian Road to collect information about work and life; and there's the most popular Habesha restaurant on that street, Marathon Restaurant. Across the street is an internet cafe where Gondar people gather. Meals to be had there are amazing. Why you ask? The answer is simple, they don't skimp on the amount of teff, they use plenty of it. Words can't describe the excitement I felt when I ate that injera for the first time. The cafés only serve bogus injera to its customers, but the employees are shrewdly eating the best injera. It's funny. In the afternoon, I casually stop by the cafe and chat with the employees in Amharic.

After a while it's time for the employees to have a late lunch. Some people invite me, saying '*Ennibla!*' (Hey! Let's eat together). Of course, I am a Gondere, so once or twice I flatly refuse the invitation. That's just good manners. Even so, when one of the employees says 'ennibla' again, according to Gondar etiquette, the person invited to eat should not accept the invitation so blithely, no matter how hungry you are. It is considered proper to turn down an invitation. Actually, when I was just learning about things Ethiopia, I took the invitation, 'enniba' at face value and just dug in as I was invited. Later, it came to me that I was criticized as shameless. Of course I was stung by hearing this. At first, I was completely confused about the use of this 'ennibla'. I mean, even now, I can't say that I fully understand the way people communicate about food.

The hustle of the streets, the stench that makes you want to turn away, the exhaust fumes, and the vehement vocal tones of the street guides; for sure at first, I was just fighting with the guides. Baye tricked a University of Florida archaeology student out of a large sum of money while she was conducting research in Gondar. Do you remember that time? One day, he said his mother was sick and needed medicine, so he begged the American student to pay for the medicine. She asked to see the bill, but she had just arrived in Ethiopia and knew nothing of the guides' machinations. Poor girl, she paid full price for the medicine. A little later, when I saw the bill, I thought the charges might not be possible so I called the clinic about it. Then, surprisingly, the person who answered the phone wasn't someone related to the clinic, but someone who was one of Baye's urchins. That 'clinic' never existed in the first place. This pissed me off too, and when I accused Baye and wanted to turn him in to the police, he flatly said that thieves were a kind of legitimate business. I was utterly astonished. If I say that he is just agoza (literally, goat skin, slang for lazy), Baye will get angry. Oh yeah, I couldn't forgive the fraud that the guides called 'the system' either. The fake celebrations, parties, etc., usually in places like gymnasiums. They invite tourists, offer them food and drinks, ask them to join a group dance, and so on. At the end of the party, they demand that the guests pay an exorbitant amount for the entertainment. Tourists who have just arrived in Gondar are usually caught in this 'system'. It shouldn't be tolerated. Speaking of terrible tricks, there's one more I should mention, Alex's VISA case. Why did he end up with an American woman? He subtlely cut a tiny hole in the Ye zinab libs (raincoat, slang for condom). That's what guides often do to secure their visas out of Ethiopia. It's absolutely awful.

Ah, is it time for dinner? The food on this table is a Vietnamese dish called pho. Oh, can you use chopsticks? Now I'll get you a fork and a spoon. It's delicious when you eat it with plenty of coriander. I don't eat pork anyway. It's okay, it's chicken, not pork. There is also some beef in it. My wife learned how to make pho from her best friend, Jessica who is Vietnamese. Jessica was a refugee like you, she came across the sea to England. When she was a baby, she left her homeland in the chaos after the war with her family on a boat. Luckily, the sinking boat was rescued by a Scottish fishing boat. Jessica's mother desperately held baby Jessica as she swam. Jessica has devoted herself to her studies and graduated from the University of Manchester and now lives near Cheadle Hulme. Her eldest son and my son were in the same class at primary school, so naturally we got to know them. Jessica now runs one of Cheadle Hulme's most popular cafes. She's so popular that sometimes even we can't get a seat. Come on, the pho is getting cold—'Ennibla!'

13

Reacquainted

14

Journey

Hey, stop it! Stop it, stop it! This can only end badly. I won't go so far as to say that I have no idea why you so badly want to go to Europe. Because many people around you crossed the sea to get there. Do you really envy them? And you think you can do it. I know, I may not have the right to say you should never go. Sure, a lot of others went to Europe. Dereb's younger brothers, Chuchu, and Mamush's brothers went to England. Desta's son, Yelikal went to Germany. I hear that Gizate's daughter, Tsehai, was in Holland, now she has moved to England. From Gondar you cross Sudan and Libya and then cross the ocean to Europe. But that sea is not Lake Tana, which can be seen from the hill of Wanza in your village. It's not Lake Hawassa, where we once went to together. It's a gigantic thing the likes of which you've never seen before. You suddenly approach me for a consultation—completely caught me off guard. The water in this case is not the holy water of the church, not the blessed holy water, not the water that cleanses us and heals us. If you go to Europe, I don't know how you'll survive, you're of Gondar.

There are reports in Japan. I have seen photos on the internet, too. Ships on the open seas off the coast of Libya. People, nothing but people, overflowing the decks of ships. Jostling throngs. Photographs with strained faces of refugees on vessels. Of course, there are a lot of Eritrean and Ethiopian faces in those huddled masses.

The reports are the same in Ethiopia. There's very similar news in Ethiopia, right? Shouldn't you live in Ethiopia? What? There isn't any work? You're not going to school so you can't get a job? Weren't you going through employment agencies in Addis Ababa? That came to nothing? It's not that things didn't work out, it's that you just don't feel like putting effort into finding a decent job. How about trying in this country? I know you just cling to dreams of going to Europe. As long as your heart beats your dreams of crossing over to Europe simply grow—even if they're not based on reason, rational judgment, or concrete plans. But it is natural for you and your companions to eat raw meat with plenty of *senafich* (mustard) sauce after *Fasika* (Easter). And it's just a matter of course to you to go out to musicians' bars, you and the hot-blooded young people around you.

Somehow I feel like I can't stop you anymore. Just let me give you some advice as a friend. This is what I heard. Sudan is on the good side of countries to pass through. Some of the police are troublesome but in general the people are kind and will provide food and short-term lodging for those of you who are in trouble. The problem is Libya after that. Among the *dellala* (intermediaries) who facilitate travel to

Europe are Ethiopians, Eritreans, Sudanese, Somalis and Libyans. The worst are the Ethiopian dellalas, unexpected right? A dellala doesn't care what happens to the people of his home country. Dellalas will take $1800 from you. Some women are raped by the dellalas. *If you're not exaggerating, you always exaggerate, Kawase.* I hear dellala take money from a traveler once, then added another $200 or $300 to the ticket price. When you tell him you're out of money, the dellala slashes your thigh with a knife.

You board a dilapidated ship with 200 people. But hey, they say the boat can carry 580 people, and it's flooded and ready to capsize in no time. Then, the leader on the ship tries to lighten the load by throwing people off. He starts with the big, fat people. There is no such thing as mercy, pity or compassion. Everyone is desperate to survive. They are hardheaded, coldhearted and rational in keeping the ship from capsizing. But the effort was futile. So you were thrown into the stormy sea. Those not wearing lifejackets drown. Oh, if the lifeboats would only come. Oh? you say God only knows? You should think a little more rationally. It's not the shallow water of the Qaha River, where you enter to purify yourself in Gondar to welcome the New Year. This is *the sea.* You get thrown into the sea and are floating helplessly like a leaf. Still you are lucky to be rescued by an Italian rescue team. 'Lampadusa, Lampedosa, Lampeduza', I forget the exact name of the island but many bodies are piled up on the shore. It's an unscrupulous thing to say but in my imagination I can't help but see you lying there. Of course, they don't carefully wrap the corpse in string seven times, put their hands together in prayer, *megenez,* and send you off to heaven like they do in your village.

Shall we talk about Germany where you want to end up? What do you think that is like? Yes, it is a country that many Eritreans and Ethiopians have as their final destination in their travels. You think it's paradise? Do you think that those of you who wash up breathless there will be given simple but clean housing, good food, and jobs? You know how deluded that is?

When I lived in Germany I met a lot of guys who had just arrived from Ethiopia and Eritrea. I'd meet them at the train station and out of the way places like at Ethiopian restaurants. I met and spoke with all kinds there. Ethiopians from town came to listen to my university lectures, too. When I arrived in Germany I was assigned an office that of course had a desk. But I preferred hanging around Central Station, Haftbahnhof rather than sitting in my office. Go to any central station, Bremen, Cologne, Hamburg or Frankfurt and within minutes you run into Ethiopians or Eritreans hanging out. I'd always encounter people. In Germany, of course, I often go to Ethiopian and Eritrean restaurants. On the north side of Frankfurt's Central Station, there is a cafe-restaurant named Mareb, named after the Mareb River that separates Ethiopia and Eritrea, symbolizing the division between the two countries. It's a little dirty, but it's a cafe with a certain warmth of atmosphere. There's a cheesy organ, a pentatonic tizeta like melody can be heard, and the shop is covered with pale green tiles.

Eritrea's national station broadcasts endlessly the theatrical plays at the National Theater in Asmara. It always portrays the women collecting firewood in the country. Dim lighting illuminates only the center of the stage. It's a cold atmosphere with no fancy props. But this cafe is full of Eritreans and Ethiopians and there are no borders or divisions between them. Although the atmosphere is chaotic the place is always full of energy as each one exchanges the drama of their travels, stories of their hometowns, and information necessary for life in this new world. It's not that I don't particularly like the taste of the injera here. It's nice to stand still in a corner of a restaurant where you smell the pungent spice of chili peppers, and can be in the language swirl of Tigrinya and Amharic. It's not like the *jorro tebbi's* (spy, intelligence officer) covert activity during the socialist regime, listening in on the details of everyone's stories and reporting to someone, interviewing here and writing a pronouncement about something. It just feels good to be in this familiar swirl of words. There are many people who don't order food because they don't have money, just hang in restaurants sipping *shai* (tea). It's been a while so I'm a bit mesmerized just listening to the words of a familiar language and being surrounded by the kindred spirits of my hometown. No, I'm not ashamed that I am Asian who can speak the language. When I greet them in Amharic or Tigrinya everyone is surprised and wary at first. However, I mention the names of the cities in Ethiopia and sing phrases from a familiar song. As we talk about various things, the doors to their hearts that had been heavily closed open up little by little. After that, some people tell me about the hardships of their trip as if the dam had been broken.

Many Germans are very kind. Volunteers who help refugees adapt to German society and live a decent life are called *lotse*. Originally, it meant a guide to direct ships coming to the wharf to help them anchor properly. Among them are university faculty and students, non-profit organizations, and Christian church workers. Some people will invite you to their home, to their diner table for a welcome party. Some Germans say they are kind to refugees because of a sense of guilt they carry from Hitler's time. Hitler killed many Jews, more people than

Mengistu Hailemariam did during the junta. And some, like far-right groups, rant that refugees will take people's jobs. Others say that refugees are poor people who have been driven from their homes and must be protected. Of course, things are never that simple, and actually much more complicated than we can imagine. In any case, what awaits you is the label of refugee pasted on you by people outside your own culture. However, I hear that the enthusiasm in society for accepting refugees with open arms has cooled. Are you still going?

In fact I don't know if you can really make it out there. I've been watching you for a long time just like you've been watching me. Just like you know all the good and bad about me, I think I know a little about you, too. Again, you're kind-hearted, but you're not sociable. You're not the kind of person who likes to show off. You have keen insight and can intuit others' feelings, but you're not the kind of guy who outsmarts, deceives, or does bad things to survive. If I were to say which type you are, you'd stand warm-heartedly on the sidelines in the world. You would not jump in and pursue something to its end. Even if you crossed Libya and crossed the sea and arrived in Germany, I don't know if you would be able to make it there. I've seen many in Germany who came out of Gondar and end up like the empty shell of a soul.

And in the meantime, you ended up moving to Egypt via Sudan. That is Cairo, and this is Osaka. A Skype call at 4:30 this morning and your voice sounds strangely lackluster. It's because you've lost a lot of weight. You ran into trouble because you didn't have enough money to pay for the overland transportation from Sudan to Egypt. In Cairo you met up with a few Gondar mates but you're still having trouble finding work. You have confidence in your Arabic so the language is not the issue. But now it's difficult, really hard, *please send some money, really?*. What did I tell you? How many times have I told you not to go? But in the end, I couldn't stop you. I don't think I have the right to stop you. Once in a while, when it was convenient for you, you'd come over to eat something but usually you didn't eat, you'd want to talk and hear stories about overseas trips. It's not really on me to stop you. You want to see the world that spreads far beyond the wide *Tarara* (plateau). You couldn't hold back your desires. What are you going to do now? What can I do from here?

15

Mischief of the Gods

Elder Brother's Way

I met *Aniki* (which coincidentally happens to be Japanese for elder brother), a middle-aged musician from Gondar, in the United States. His real name is Setegn Atenaw. The territory of Aniki's musical activities is U Street in the northwestern part of Washington, D.C.; it is also the center of social life and economic activity for Ethiopian immigrants. One day as I was walking down this street I heard the faint sound of a familiar stringed instrument, the masenqo, mixed with the sound of an electronic organ coming from the second floor of a building. It's an earthy, if somewhat difficult string sound played on a goat-skinned resonator with strings made of horse tail hair. It is a nostalgic and lovely sound familiar to Ethiopia that almost gets buried by the electronic instruments accompanying it, but he is clearly a very skilled player. My chest swells upon hearing this music and invited by the sound of these strings I climb the stairs. In a bar-like space several Ethiopian looking musicians were tuning up. They stare at me suspiciously. For openers in Amharic I greet a smallish man dressed in brightly colored clothes sitting on a chair playing masenqo. However, after giving me an annoyed look as if to tell me not to disturb their practice, he continued playing as if I weren't even there. The tense atmosphere worsened. In Gondar the one playing the masenqo would be of Azmari origins. As a long-time acquaintance of the Azmaris, I speak their language, which is more of a jargon, slang or code than language proper. It is a code shared by them to talk in-group and exclude non Azmaris. So I tried Azmari on the one playing the masenqo. '*Denichi naw Suruiyo conti naw kamunukeno yowaiyuh gobbilaye Sunke degmo zata negne*' (Hello. How's your work going? What village are you from? I'm your brother). His eyes widened instantly and his expression brightened as if the sun had broken through the clouds. 'Why do you know our language? Who taught you?' After talking to him, I learned that this masenqo player was from an Azmari village north of Gondar, where I had lived. I had often heard that one of the village elder's sons, who was said to be a master of masenqo, had gone to the United States and never returned. This old man often lamented to me: 'My son hasn't come home for 20 years.' I certainly never thought I would run into his son in the United States. Setegn Atenaw kept asking me how his relatives were doing and welcomed me as if he had been reunited with his kin for the first time in a long time. 'Don't stay in a hotel. Come to my house, you're my brother'. Shortly after meeting Aniki, I canceled my hotel room and moved into his cramped apartment. And so began a short but pleasant few months I spent with Aniki.

Aniki was born thirty-four kilometers south of Gondar in an Azmari village called Bahir Gimb. It is a small village consisting of about 17 households. Long before I met Aniki, I had a house built in this village and lived there to research local musicial activities. Aniki learned from his father to sing and play by ear when he was a kid and by the age of 20 he had become a fairly well-known singer in the streets of Gondar. It was the era of military rule. Aniki toured various parts of Ethiopia as a member of a band called Qinat, whose musicians were from across Ethiopia. Qinat played a role in conveying socialist ideology to the common people through traditional performing arts. In the early 1990s, Aniki went to Canada as a member of an Ethiopian traditional performing arts band. He fled the troupe and then moved to the United States from Canada. Disappearance and exile of dancers and singers during tours in Europe and the United States were by no means uncommon.

If you walk down U Street, you will see many shops run by Ethiopian immigrants with signs in Amharic. Here, you can eat injera made from teff harvested in Idaho and at the club where Aniki works as a musician, you can enjoy a flashy folk dance show that compares favorably with such shows in Ethiopia. There are Ethiopian real estate companies, hair salons, and music stores. Propaganda vans touting concerts by Ethiopian musicians on tour in the United States pass by, and leaders of the opposition party from Addis Ababa come to campaign. It is impossible to talk about the political economy, artistic and cultural dynamics of Ethiopia today without mentioning the investment and influence of the 500,000 Ethiopian immigrants in North America on their homeland.

A large number of Ethiopians emigrated due to the rise of the military regime and the massacre of citizens in the 1970s, and drought and famine in the middle of the 1980s. From the latter half of the 1970s, many from Gondar fled to Europe and the United States via Sudan and Eritrea. The majority of those who immigrated to North America settled in large cities such as Washington, D.C., New York, Los Angeles, Seattle, Houston, and Atlanta. Gondar immigrants who initially worked in the service industry and manual labor gradually opened restaurants, pharmacies, real estate agencies, accounting firms, travel agencies, beauty salons and boutiques. At the same time Ethiopian Orthodox churches were established throughout the United States, and Gondar mutual aid organizations were formed in each city. Since the transition to the democratic administration in the 1990s, there has been a dramatic increase in the number of people going to the United States through a visa system (referred to by Ethiopians as the 'DV lottery') that promotes cultural diversity. In the city men and women of all ages talk about their dreams of moving abroad.

Aniki has a song in his repertoire, 'The Good Immigrant', it is an ironic song about that trend among the people of Gondar and by extension Ethiopians who move and aspire to move abroad.

Hey Ethiopians
leaving Ethiopia used to mean death
wrapped in sorrow and anxiety
with a dark feeling
leave the homeland
leave the relatives
went abroad

what happened to that now
as soon as you get your passport and visa
drink, eat, sing and dance
party after party
what it means to immigrate
it's like a happy wedding [4]

The behavior of those returning from Europe and the United States is probably one of the reasons why the trend of glorifying overseas migration got started in Gondar. For example, someone in Washington, D.C. who runs a cleaning business and just makes ends meet, then returns to Gondar after a long absence. In 'decorating your hometown', you show off to your relatives and friends and help create the image of 'foreign emigrants as successful' which then spreads as a matter of course. Seeing the prosperity of those who have returned home to Gondar, hearing their rose-colored success stories, it's then a forgone conclusion that not envying them would be a mistake.

Aniki has been invited to perform masenqo at festivals such as weddings and banquets of Ethiopian immigrants, and at cultural events that promote unity in the Ethiopian community. He has been invited to perform in Atlanta, Portland and Seattle, anywhere there is a large Gondar community. Like Aniki, there are several musicians in the Washington, D.C. area who are of Azmari roots. Aniki's distant relatives, who were also born in the village of Gondar, hide their origins for fear of the discrimination against Azmari musicians following them. Instead they claim to be modern artists although they too are masters of masenqo. They avoid playing this stringed instrument that has become a symbol of the group and carries a certain stigma. They stick to the image of singers in a band with electronic instruments. Aniki, on the other hand, insists on singing along with the masenqo, an instrument he has been playing since childhood. Certainly, just like in their home country, Ethiopian immigrants sometimes look coldly at masenqo performers. In fact, I once heard Aniki being ridiculed by some in the audience during a masenqo performance. But Aniki knows better. The earthy, wild, rough sounds of this simple stringed instrument remind the Gondar people of the rugged and magnificent highlands of northern Ethiopia, of the teff fields shining in the sunshine, and of their friends and relatives back home.

The range of Aniki's art is wide. He plays with taste and effortlessly the esoteric songs of Medina, Begena and other locations which explain the frailty of life and futility of materialism delivered through meta-phorical expressions. He also has in his repertoire bogus lyrics of Bob Marley songs. On top of that he has a habit of swinging his hips during performances and the audience bursts into laughter. He's totally a comical, funny clown in the Azmari ancient tradition. However, I will never forget the shock of hearing him perform at the Ethiopian music club called Ibex. He connects an amplifier to the masenqo to amplify and create distortion in the stringed instrument's sound. He repeats a short phrase endlessly, and then goes into a solo that sounds like a ferocious serpent writhing. He seems to draw the listener into a dangerous, luscious groove. I have listened to hundreds of Azmari performances, but no Azmari can extend the range of masenqo and add a variety of colors to the sound like Aniki. It is easy to understand why his musician colleagues call him 'King of Masenqo'.

At dawn after his performance, he ate in the Adams Morgan neighborhood and drove his car home past the Pentagon. After a hard day it's time to take a breather. He listens to me talk about what is going on in Gondar villages and towns, laughs and cries at my jokes about village farmers and livestock. The stories are never ending. However, when Aniki interacts with me no matter how much he smiles, he always comes to his senses and a sober look returns to his face, 'This is a land of immoral people. We just pray and sing to God'. In his small apartment he offers me, the guest, his large bed and he curls up on the sofa in his living room. He wakes up at noon and eats a late breakfast. He sautés red pepper, spices, and plenty of finely chopped beef in lots of butter in a frying pan and eats it with injera. This dish is called *kitfo*. Of course even if I warned him that he would definitely get sick if he only ate this kind of food every morning, he wouldn't listen. Before eating people always make the sign of the cross and pray while looking up to the sky. In addition, he does not forget to sincerely pray to God to protect him and his younger brother. I suddenly thought, 'how does it feel to hear about a hometown you haven't returned to in 20 years?' In the end I never heard why he couldn't or wouldn't go back to his hometown.

Aniki struts down U Street in clown-like operatic flamboyance. He shoulders me aside as if to tell me 'shut up and follow' and pops into the shops of Ethiopian peers, greets acquaintances affably and makes small talk. At first I thought he was just boasting to me and about the breadth of his circle of friends. However it later dawned on me that this was a theatrical sales activity, the gathering information and self-promotion for more performance opportunities.

Spending a few hours in the markets and cafes of Ethiopian immigrants on U Street makes me feel like I'm back in Gondar. But before Ethiopian immigration increased, U Street was a densely populated African-American neighborhood and is still quite racially diverse. When I walk with Aniki, I hear sardonic comments as we pass others, 'What's this guy wearing? You insane?' ... 'Check this fucker out'. Aniki doesn't take it laying down either, 'Shut up nigger. Get outta my face'. Aniki fights back when such comments should just be ignored. Aniki only speaks limited, broken English but seems to have quite a good vocabulary when it comes to insults and he puts it on display at times like this. I was horrified at this and thought it could end in a fight. I was also horrified that he would walk in and out of a *khat bet* without hesitation.

In Ethiopia, Kenya, Djibouti, Yemen, among other places, *khat* is just a weak stimulant and luxury item. In North America, however, it is a fully controlled substance. Some of the Ethiopian immigrant-owned general stores in Washington, D.C. have khat bets. A narrow corridor extends from the side of the cash register, you go through it, open some heavy doors and reach the basement. It is difficult to import fresh leaves, so dried khat powder called '*khat aweza*' is used. This pale green powder is dissolved in hot water and drunk, or it can be mixed with alcohol. Aniki brought me into this place. In this dark and suspicious space, there are seven or eight men. They're heavyset and are full of tattoos. They stare at me with bloodshot eyes. Aniki, who seems to be a regular customer, smiles and introduces me to everyone as his younger brother. They all seem to be Ethiopian immigrants, but one person seems to be Sudanese. The customers never let their guard down when I, an Asian, suddenly entered this secret space. Regardless of my uncomfortable and unpleasant feelings Aniki smiles and laughs while ruminating about upcoming performances, and U Street rumors. Even if I greet them in Amharic or Tigrinya, their hostile gazes don't change and the air seems heavy and stagnant. 'Why did you ever live in Ethiopia? What were you doing in Ethiopia?' 'Are you a spy?' Even though I regretted that I had come to this place, I politely answered each and every one of their hostile questions.

One time we were strolling down U Street and I was about to stop by a Starbucks. Aniki said, 'This is a place for tourists and foreigners. Stop!' Aniki who the hell are you in this country?' We looked each in the eye and grinned.

The fun days with Aniki passed quickly. It was time to leave U Street. like a bird (*wefi naw*) soaring from earth into sky. It's the farewell in the style of Gondar people on the road. In the first place Gondar people highly value their relationships with others and are quick to empathize with others. At times, especially when it comes to their neighbors, they tend to go overboard meddling in others' affairs. And yet, could it be possible that they cut off their attachments and depart immediately in circumstances like these? No, perhaps the full understanding of one another's sentimental disposition gives birth to a thoughtful attention to others—so, whether offered a meal or the one being left behind is going on and on speaking—when the time comes the one taking leave just departs. There is no need for sticky words of gratitude between those who are deeply connected.

That evening, I wandered into the bar where Aniki plays every week as usual. I intended to briefly say goodbye to Aniki, who I was indebted to and head straight to the airport. But no matter how long I wait, he never comes. I ask the waitress, 'How's Aniki doing today?' He didn't tell me until the end that he works in a parking lot a few days a week. Besides playing, he must have felt ashamed that he was making a living doing part-time jobs.

After leaving the store and wandering around U Street thinking about what to do, Aniki suddenly appeared in front of me. He was in tears. Without a word he shoved some crumpled US dollar bills into my jacket pocket. It must have been all the money he had at that moment. 'Stop that, I don't need it?' 'No, you should take it'. 'No, I said I don't need it'. 'No, you take it!'

16

The Crucifix

'Touch me, on the forehead, on the cheek, on the lips'.

What you see inside the glass cases is always the same boring stuff. One is surrounded by cases with various masks, colorful clothes, and many other objects brought from Africa. Fellow Ethiopians are standing still looking around a tiny exhibition space. There's a couple holding hands, an ordinary elderly lady, a worker who came to change the lights, children with pens and notebooks—these are the people I observe passing by me today. When I first came to this museum, the place was bustling with people and activity. That's just in the past few years—now it's become a church that's lost its prayers.

'Touch me, on the forehead, on the cheek, on the lips'. I whisper casting a spell on people passing by, but no one can hear me, let alone looks at me. Even if I were to break through this glass case and expose my true feelings, no one would know all the formalities that surround me. No one will pay homage to me, no one will touch me.

A man who knows my hometown very well seems to live on the fourth floor of this building. But he doesn't usually come to see me or touch me. Next door to me is a rather strange person I have named 'K6907'. He's like something in the Ethiopian Geez Old Testament. He complains about me every day: 'This incompetent anthropologist is the reason why we Abyssinian families are confined, prisoners in a narrow glass case in this bleak museum, that's a church that has lost its prayers'. This man doesn't know anything about my master, Priest Abba Fikermariam, or how I should be treated, properly.

There are gods from all over Ethiopia with familiar shapes that I met when I walked around the countryside with Priest Abba Fikermariam. The gods are made of stone or wood and laid out in lines on their sides in storage cases where for a long time they have been mere objects with no prayers or respect given to them, just labeled with catalogue numbers.

Speaking of which, this afternoon a group of children wearing yellow hats passed in front of me. One girl suddenly stopped in front of me and her eyes fixed on me a moment. Her transparent eyes seemed a little mischievous, but they were full of kindness. It was a strange look. I couldn't tell if she was looking at me or looking at the world beyond me. It was as if shepherds caught in a sudden downpour wrapped themselves in thick plastic bags and crouched down while waiting for the rain to pass. It was like the kind eyes of a priest when he praised me calling me a priest-in-the-making after I recited a long prayer that I had put to memory. At that moment, for the first time in a long time my heart throbbed. But the girl quickly turned her eyes from me and ran back to her circle of friends.

A dauntingly long time ago I walked all over the open plateau—across rivers, over hills, across rivers again, over hills again with Priest Abba Fikermariam. We sometimes took busses and also rocked back and forth on the back of a mule. The priest pressed me to the foreheads, cheeks, and lips of the people we met along the way: a woman carrying a large water jug on her back; a girl collecting dry cow dung for fuel—they stopped walking and would kneel before me. There was a beggar who was dying from a serious skin disease who was deeply relieved by my touch, and a demon-possessed boy was brought before the priest, trembling all over, foaming from the mouth and repeating something incomprehensible. After the priest sprinkled the boy with tsabal (holy water), he gently pressed me to his forehead and said a prayer. Then the boy came to his senses as if nothing had been wrong. Yes, as if nothing at all had happened. I have also met many mediums who practice zar, what the Orthodox church calls the religion of Satan. They perform a zar or beckon a qole (spirit) and the medium becomes possessed and asks the qole for advice. The medium was given various tributes such as sheep, beans, and perfume, and everyone danced in ecstasy. More than one qole descends to one medium. Each of them has a name, gender, home, and temperament. They fly across the sky from uninhabited *bereha* (wastelands), lakes and forests. Yes, there are various religions among these people. Some are Muslim, others are devout Orthodox believers. Some people have memorized the entire Old Testament. Unbelievable? But some Orthodox monks hesitate to join a zar. All who are astray or mad, can be made right by touching my potent, powerful body, they are blessed.

People invite us into their homes, take off the priest's shoes, wash his feet thoroughly with their hands, and kiss the feet respectfully. Then again the priest turns things over to me by pressing me against people's foreheads, cheeks and lips. Thousands, or tens of thousands of times, I have proudly touched people's skin, with my potent and powerful body and in that blessed them.

Crucified on a cross many times larger than my body, Jesus was stabbed all over with spears and bled profusely. The Angel Urael caught the blood that flowed from Jesus and spread it all over the world. An Orthodox church was built where the blood of Jesus fell. Yes, of course the blood continues to drip—here, there and over there—can't you see the blood? Which voice is Saint Michael's? Can't you hear the voice of Saint Gabriel? You don't know about Kristos Samra or her miracles? Of course you know about the penance of Tekle Haymanot, right? A gentle relief of the suffering of Jesus is at the heart of Orthodox rituals. You don't seem to know anything. Same as the anthropologist in charge of Abyssinia at this museum.

This place where I am currently trapped, must be a place like Libanos before Saint Giorgis visited. It is a land of heretics with no respect for God, with no prayers. Yes, I'm sure it is. I am going to tell you a story that I have heard many times from priests. It's about how (Orthodox) Christianity spread to Libanos, the land of heretics. Priests have told the story over and over again to children who come to church.

In the land of Libanos there lived a dragon that breathed fire and had large wings. People used to worship this dragon. The dragon was controlled by a demon called Satinael, and had a daily routine of eating girls, offerings made by people. The dragon ate the girl's flesh and drank her blood. This custom continued for many years. One day while traveling on horseback, Giorgis met a girl tied to a tree waiting to be eaten by a dragon. Giorgis is suspicious of the girl's appearance, she tells him that she is destined to be eaten by a dragon and that he too would fall prey, she warned. But Giorgis didn't run away, 'I will fight for you'. The dragon came and saw Giorgis, became furious and attacked him. Giorgis carved a crucifix and offered a prayer: *'Besmaab weweld wemenfes kidus, ahadu amlak'* (In the name of God, God the Father, Son, Holy Spirit). At that moment the power of the dragon suddenly weakened. Giorgis strangled the weakened dragon with a rope. Then he used his spear to stab the dragon. After the thrusts of the spear the dragon dies. Dudianos, the King of Libanos, was delighted at the slaying of the dragon but he became furious when he learned that Giorgis was in Libanos preaching a new religion, Orthodox Christianity. Giorgis was imprisoned. The king poisoned Giorgis, chopped him up, set him on fire, drowned him in water and subjected him to all sorts of torture. But Giorgis survived all these torments many times over thanks to the power of God. Every time Giorgis went through an additional torture, the number of Orthodox Christians grew in Libanos. King Dudianos smashed Giorgis to pieces as one would threshing grain, Giorgis' body was powder and scattered floating in the air, carried by the wind, and it attached to plants. All the plants that were dusted began to shout, 'Giorgis, Giorgis, Giorgis, Giorgis!'—the plants of the world sang the name of Giorgis. That would have been an amazing sight! Then powdered Giorgis was naturally gathered into one place, regained his original form and revived. The discouraged King Dudianos finally converted to Orthodox Christianity and began to believe in God.

If the priest were here now and told this story to the children with the yellow hats, how would they react? I'm sure it would make everyone's eyes sparkle. I say without hesitation, 'Touch your forehead to mine, your cheek to mine, your lips to mine'. Will the day come when Giorgis comes to save my chained body?

Our church is located on a small hill in the center of Gondar.

You can hear the voices of children singing *mezmurs* (hymns) to the Blessed Virgin Mary, and the chants of priests and their companions. '*Besmaab weweld wemenfes kidus, ahadu amlak*' (In the name of God, God the Father, Son, Holy Spirit). The hyena's voice that I hear at night echoes in my ears. The fragrant wood that purifies the body and the fragrant smell of the inside of the gourd container come back to me. Why smoke a gourd? A fourth-floor anthropologist would have dismissed it simply, 'to sterilize'. But that explanation is superficial and sloppy. Fill the gourd with freshly squeezed milk. And the scent of smoked gourd mixes with the milk. Yes, it will be a taste that everyone in the land will love, and that the priests will love more than anything else. In a word, it would be the taste of my hometown. And the fleshy and warm hands of the priest, but that was a daunting past that happened far away from this glass case, 'please touch me on the forehead, on the cheeks, on the lips'.

17

The Ethiopia Hotel

I'm back inside you again, like a yo-yo that rotates and moves up and down repeatedly. I have repeated the endless movement with you, coming back and leaving, coming back and leaving. Inside this movement I have spoken words, used images, talked again and again about how fascinating you are, and even thought about myself sometimes. But have those thoughts, those words and images reached you, even once?

Built by the Italian army, a base for movies, plays, karate club tournaments, recitals—a wealth of entertainments for the citizens. Across the square, you can see the royal palaces that tell of the prosperity of the Solomon dynasty and the Gondar period. Next to this, an enormous fig tree in Jan Tekele Park, has watched over the city for hundreds of years. The people of Gondar have a special affection for this tree. Like the legs of a giant spider, the branches extend in all directions, block the strong sunlight of the plateau and provide a shade and space for lovers to relax. There is a Gondar proverb: when the branch of the giant tree in Jan Tekele Park stretches out and touches the soil, a girl beckons a boy to come over to her.

In the mid-1930s, Italian soldiers left an Art Deco-ish hotel in the middle of the city. This is my regular hotel, the Ethiopia Hotel. There is a restaurant on the first floor and about twenty guest rooms on the second floor. While the building looks elegant and strong from the outside, the inside is old and rickety. Looking out from the entrance, diagonally to the right is Room 11. The cone-shaped building built by the Italian army has peeling ceiling panels, stains on walls, broken windows, shards of broken glass on the floor and smells of clogged drains. I know you are welcoming me through those various signals. As soon as I entered the room and before opening my suitcase, I lay on my back on the bed under the ceiling fan. I flew about 10,000 kilometers from Japan, arrived in Addis Ababa. From there I traveled 730 kilometers north, crossed Lake Tana, the source of the Blue Nile, came to you where I look down at the magnificent plateau. The scene keeps my arrogance in check. As I immerse myself in the noise of the city that fills the room, my body and mind dissolve. I feel myself gradually synchronizing with the street that invades through the thin walls. For a while I try to think back on what I planned to do in this city before that arduous trip. I am enveloped in a whirlpool of sounds, all preparations have disappeared from my mind. The faces of my friends on the street invade it. When that happens, my heart begins to float. I can't stand it anymore. So I get up and leave the room. The odor of the paint on the toilet and the floor mix together, the concoction that is the characteristic stench of this place. I hold my breath and quickly run through the narrow corridor. I run down the stairs leading to the hotel entrance, I pass Ehetnesh, a hotel employee, on the landing of the stairs. She holds a silver tray of injera in one hand, room service for guests. The side dish on the tray is *dulet*, which is stir-fried beef or sheep organs. I greet her pompously but politely, and eat the injera as if a bird of prey pouncing on a small terrestrial animal. Ehetnesh tells me to stop, I flash an embarrassed smile. I'm back, my heart mutters.

Leaning against the door frame of the hotel's entrance, I gazed out at the street. The midday sun is shining brightly. The number of auto tricycles swirling through the streets has increased considerably.Across the street is the laundry run by Hasen. Addisu and others are encamped next to it. Shoes are stacked a meter high, Addisu sits in the middle, 'I'm still repairing shoes today'. Addisu loves gambling, alcohol, and his favorite leaf, khat. Two front teeth are missing because he had a fight with an acquaintance over a woman. He is sometimes called, 'Soccer Goal' because of missing teeth. His prime seat under the Pepsi billboard is a great vantage point for the busy crossroads. He sits here, oversees the city, and makes a living by shining and mending shoes. He says, 'From the day I first came to town, then the day I returned after a long absence and up till now I work hard from morning to night to feed my children'. Addisu is also a data bank of the latest information on the city. From the details of a road expansion plan be considered at City Hall, to a bribery scandal surrounding the mayoral election, to the fights between the in-laws at home—all sorts of gossip accumulates within him. From politicians to thief bosses, all sorts of people come to collect information from him. That's why he's a recognized persona all over his world.

'Hey Addisu, long time no see, how are you?' 'Kawase, how are you doing? You never call me at all'. The soot of the street on Addisu's thick skin and being greeted by his toothless smile fill me with joy. I'm back!

My relationship to these streets has not always been easygoing. In that connection I must mention Babbie, a lonely orphan who wandered the streets, and a regular guest of Room 11. He used to come to me, Addisu and others. Babbie treated me like an older brother, supported me every step of the way in my research in this city and the villages on the outskirts of the city. Although he had never received a formal education, there was no research assistant who understood my thoughts as deeply as he did and helped me with my field work as much as him. Cheerful, curious, and talkative like the torrential rains of the month of *Hamle*. He pulled all sorts of pranks. He loves to play with my equipment, especially my video camera. In fact he worked as an assistant in many shootings. Once as a prank, he filmed his own genitals, recording over a video of rituals that I had painstakingly filmed. When I found the footage, I scolded Babbie so much that he became depressed. The ritual tape was rendered useless. However, even as I got angry at Babbie's mischief, I think I enjoyed his adventures from the bottom of my heart.

One day in Room 11, he spoke passionately about making a decision to go to school. Although he was starting late, it was not too late, and I was delighted with his decision. I paid for his education and some living expenses, and sent him money. It was not easy for me as a student. Whenever I returned to Gondar, Babbie thanked me and happily told me about his schoolmates and teachers. 'Has it been two and a half years?' A friend of Babbie's informed me that he had not been to school at all since he started receiving money from me. It was a story that I did not want to believe. When I visited the school, I found no evidence that he had attended. My anger at being betrayed by Babbie, whom I had deeply trusted, was intense. He never explicitly told me why he didn't go to school. We became estranged after that, and we never saw each other except in passing on the street a few times. Street people in Gondar often say, 'Meeting people brings joy and pain at the same time'.

'Welcome home'.
'Hello. Long time no see'.
'How are you? Has it been a year?'
'No, about eight months'.

I've been engaged with this city for a long time. It's wild to think of all the emotions that have run through me because of it. I have heard countless gunshots, cries and shouts of joy. When the Italian soldiers withdrew from this city they did it all at once. There was a woman gazing off into the distance, a tremendous distance. The officer's words, as he touched her baby's cheek gently, he said he would see her again soon. Kind words and full of love, but she knew. That it was a farewell forever. That baby is now the old man who runs the Dashen General Store where you buy potato chips and canned tuna from the Middle East. Sitting on a chair in the back of the store counting the bills is the big guy everyone calls Bambino. More than 30 years after the end of Italian rule, the era of 'red terror' came in the form of a military government with socialist ideology. A group of soldiers led by the tyrant Melaku Teferra mercilessly opened fire on the demonstrators who were organized by university students on this street in front of us, turning the streets red with the blood of unarmed youths. The laments and cries of the parents who came to pick up the bodies echoed in the streets. Relatives had to pay the soldiers to take the bodies of their sons. One of the soldiers from that incident who pierced the young man's heart is a middle-aged gentleman who ran an Internet cafe just down the hill. He's always happy to see me back in town from Japan, and he happily asks questions about Japanese electrical appliances and all. Something beyond good and evil governs the destinies of the people of these streets, sometimes connecting people and sometimes pulling them apart. I can't do anything about it. I am nothing more than an orchestrator, quietly accompanying people's sorrows and joys'. 'Of course, I also remember when you first came to this city. I can see you entering Room 11 for the first time along with the fleas and ticks that you picked up on the long-distance bus. The activities of the people on the street which you soon became fascinated with, seemed too rich and poisonous at first. Blocking out the voices of the young people on the street who yell and tease you. I see you walking quickly down the street, returning to this room with a sullen face and a closed heart, thin as a candle and barely able to speak the language'.

'I also remember your happy companions: Mulu who likes to draw; Tigabu and other child musicians; Tomo who came to study architecture from Tokyo; Addisu who is your best friend and shoeshine man. And just how much time did you spend, you and you alone in Room 11?

Speaking of friends, yes, Babbie. I know you are quick to think about him these days, even though you try to avoid thinking about him as much as possible. Even if your friends on the street ask you about him, you won't give a clear answer and will change the subject and skirt the issue. Without mistake you have your faults too. If you really wanted to support him, you should have done more. It was tragic to see him cut off his bond with you. Like a husk, he wandered around the streets and became addicted to alcohol and cigarettes. Occasionally, he curses you abusively and sends you nasty emails or makes phone calls. You stubbornly shut him out and refused to listen to his heartfelt cries for a long time. However, now that it's been some time, you think it may be okay to meet him and have a long talk'.

The streets of Gondar sing, dance, rage, sob and meander. The streets shout with joy, yawn, play tricks, sigh, and tell lies. The streets live, die, shrink, stretch, surge, pop, tumble, leap and roll. Even if you are far away the streets will invade your memory, diffuse into the future, condense, dissolve, shift the earth's axis, the time axis, and continue to shake you. With the spirits of the streets, I, too, will waltz on the tizeta scale—so the streets reach deep inside you, properly.

17

The Ethiopia Hotel

Mischief of the Gods

Mischief of the Gods

Epilogue

Why is it that we are so attracted to the words and actions of people who at first glance seem irrational and inexplicable? Not only do they push me to imagine the multi-layered nature of the world, but they are also an attraction that lure me into unknown horizons and encourage me to internal transformations.

This book is an attempt to get closer, sing together, and tell stories about the people I have met and interacted with in the streets of Gondar, Ethiopia and elsewhere. The stories are also a vehicle for experimentation with narrative form. The sighs of the helpless, the will to live, the strength in the shadow of death—on the street, they approach me in clear outlines and colors and invade me. The street is also a subject that I have sympathy for, that manifests in me, that changes shape, changes appearance, sometimes permanently changing.

Many chapters in this book have been significantly revised based on stories in the evening edition of the *Kyoto Shimbun* newspaper series 'Modern Words', published from 2014 to 2016. In addition, chapters 2, 10, 14, 15, and 17 are newly written for this book.

First of all, I would like to express my gratitude to the *Kyoto Shimbun* for giving me the opportunity to create this book. Around the end of the summer of 2016, I received a proposal from the publisher Sekai Shisosha to compile these stories. This book would not have originally been possible without the valuable advice and tenacious support of everyone at Sekai Shisosha. I want to thank them from the bottom of my heart.

Finally, to my friends of Gondar. I don't dare apologize for my absence. Because at this very moment, I walk with you on the street that stretches out in front of the Ethiopia Hotel, together we sing and dance. Next time I visit Gondar, shall I treat you to mead, the usual shop? In years when we didn't have much honey, we went to that store that added a little sugar to mead. An Azmari with a stringed masenqo might come by and sing and put us in a good mood. Or maybe make us feel awkward by singing and making jokes that strike too close to home. Well that'd be just fine. Exceptionally sweet and sour mead. Let's hope the taste hasn't changed much when we visit the place.

Notes

1. Mesffin Messele. 2000. Abbaude Oral Poetry in South Wollo: A Descriptive Analysis. A thesis Submitted to the School of Graduate Studies of Addis Ababa University for the Degree of Master of Arts in Literature

2. Pessoa Poetry Collection. 2008. Translated by Nao Sawada. Kaigai Poetry Bunko 16, Shichosha Publishing (in Japanese).

3. Itsushi Kawase. 2012. The Azmari Performance During Zar Ceremonies in Northern Gondar, Ethiopia -Challenges and Prospects for the Documentation-, CULTURES SONORES D'AFRIQUE V, publie sous la direction de Junzo Kawada, Yokohama: Institut de Recherches sur les Cultures Populaires du Japon, pp. 65-80.

4. Solomon Addis Getahun.2006. The History of Ethiopian Immigrants and Refugees in America, 1900-2000: Patterns of Migration, Settlement, Survival and Adjustment. New York: LFB Scholarly Publishing LLC.

Notes

Printed in the USA
CPSIA information can be obtained
at www.ICGtesting.com
LVHW071318150324
774517LV00059B/2696